I AM A PROMISE

I AM A PROMISE
the school achievement of British African Caribbeans

Yvonne Channer

Trentham Books

First published in 1995 by Trentham Books Limited

Trentham Books Limited
Westview House
734 London Road
Oakhill
Stoke-on-Trent
Staffordshire
England ST4 5NP

British Cataloguing in Publication Data
A catalogue record for this book is available from the British Library
ISBN: 1 85856 038 1

Cover illustration by Steve Martin
(from an idea by Henry Russell Channer)

Designed and typeset by Trentham Print Design Ltd., Chester and printed in Great Britain by BPC Wheatons Ltd., Exeter

Contents

Foreword

This book examines an interesting phenomenon which has received little attention. Many recent government reports, other publications and media reports have documented *ad infinitum* the apparent academic failure of African-Caribbean British children. A plethora of articles, research papers and books have probed varying aspects of this apparent failure.

This has caused me considerable concern, because much of the data presented sits uneasily with my experience and knowledge of the British African-Caribbean society. Although I had attended a comprehensive school in which the scenario described by Wright (1988) was evident, (most black children in lower streams etc) I was also conscious that other sections of African-Caribbean society seemed to be having a different experience. I could readily recall a number of my African-Caribbean friends, family members and acquaintances who did not match the data presented by researchers. An albeit superficial calculation suggested that many of the individuals whose academic progress was at odds with current research findings were of the same or similar religious persuasion as myself — ie Seventh-Day Adventist or other black-led religious denominations. It appeared that some of these individuals had 'underachieved' at school and moved on to periods of unemployment or manual or semi-skilled work before returning to the academic arena. Others obtained the necessary exam results at school or at Further Education Colleges.

To test out the accuracy of such impressions it was important to examine numerical evidence which would either support or refute my observations. A number of questions appeared central to the discussion: for example to what extent were the individuals who are at the source of this debate — ie African-Caribbean religious achievers — different from other African-Caribbeans? Were they representative and typical of African-Caribbeans in England? Could these questions be answered by statistical data?

Conversations with statisticians led me to believe that it was difficult if not impossible to produce a rigorous statistical study, given the lack of essential data, whereas an ethnographic approach offered an opportunity to unravel the views and perceptions of the individuals involved. Despite the implication that the final choice of research method was as a result of default, like Plummer (1980) I conclude that the life history technique is at its best when it is being used in an exploratory fashion for generating a range of concepts.

The structure of this book is the result of much debate. I was clear that my foreshadowing ideas about the possible role and impact of religion on the lives of African-Caribbean should not be imposed on the subjects. They should be permitted the freedom to 'tell their story'. However, leaving the sociological analysis of the replies to the last quarter of the study could result in an inconclusive end to the work. Accordingly, the early discussion of religion should be seen as factual and theoretical underpinning of one possible dimension of the debate.

This book gives them that freedom — and their story is one to which teachers, educational planners and parents should pay serious attention.

Acknowledgements

This book has been completed because of the considerable generosity, encouragement, interest and support of many people.

Before I list the human assistance I would like to acknowledge God's guidance in locating relevant information and giving inspiration from the beginning to the completion of this study.

I am especially thankful to Sandra Henry who showed much patience in the typing of the material. Without the co-operation and participation of the respondents, this book would not exist. I thank them for their involvement.

My church family and friends as well as my husband Henry and children Russell and Maria have given me much support and encouragement.

Finally, the role played by Dr J Quicke and Dr Petronella Breinburg during my period of registration at the University has been central to the ongoing tasks and final completion of the thesis.

Chapter 1

Current Affairs

Introduction

Much of the debate in the past three decades concerning the educational experiences of pupils of Caribbean backgrounds in England, has centred around the concept of 'underachievement'. A number of studies and research projects which examine this area of education conclude by observing that for a variety of reasons, British children of Caribbean descent are failing to achieve their academic potential in the educational system. This chapter considers the appropriateness and usefulness of this concept, noting the misleading message it is likely to present. After giving some space to this discussion, the chapter outlines a number of studies undertaken during the past thirty years which present evidence and explanations for the view that black children are 'failing' in British schools. These include psychogenic and sociogenic factors, advanced as explanations for this phenomenon. A number of recent studies examine notable factors of interest in the relationship between black children and their teachers as well as wider school and post school experiences.

For the past decade there has been some consensus that the term 'black' should be used to describe people who are unfavourably treated in British (and other societies) because of their colour. Nick's use of the term was intended to indicate a collective pride and sense of positive identity. There is an ongoing debate (see Modood, 1988) about the appropriateness of a term which purely defines a person in terms of problems. Although it can be viewed as a political statement which is evaluative and inspirational and unites many different groups of radically oppressed people, Modood argues that most ordinary people wish to be defined in terms of a historically received identity, a distinctive set of beliefs and practices.

An underlying theme in this discussion is the impact of covert and overt racism on the lives of black children and their families. However, the chapter concludes by identifying a general tendency in the previously mentioned research projects to focus on the issues of oppression, thus neglecting discussion about the resources and means of resistance available to black children and their families. My reason for commencing this book, one which considers the notion of academic achievement, with a literature review chapter on academic underachievement, is to demonstrate that there has been relatively little movement in this area of debate. The underachievement debate has monopolised the agenda, resulting in a somewhat stagnant discussion which mainly considers negative experiences and rarely explores the potential of coping strategies. Education researchers who have begun to examine notions of resistance and methods of surviving in a racist society (Mac an Ghaill, 1988. Gillborn, 1990) have provided me with a launching pad for future debate.

There follows a historical outline which not only sets the scene for a discussion about black children in British schools but is also an essential back-drop or reference point throughout the chapter and the book. Education provision can be viewed as being systematically related to the social scene and as such is an area which mirrors the forces in society. As a function of society education cannot, in an isolated fashion, control its practice without reference to the socio-economic and political milieu. The following review of literature which explores the role and nature of education as it impacts on children of Caribbean descent highlights the need for this to be placed within a wider socio-political and historical context.

Historical overview

Walvin (1973) notes that as early as the 15th century, the presence of black people in Britain warranted anxious comments from no less than Her Majesty Queen Elizabeth I. The situation was thus: 'hunger swept the land, England was faced by a problem which taxed the resources of government to the limits', and that 'immigrants added to the problem, since no group was so immediately visible as the blacks'. Due to England's involvement in the slave trade thousands of black people were living English cities. Queen Elizabeth is said to have written to the Lord Mayors of the country's major cities:

> there are of late divers blackamore brought into the realm, of which kind of people there are already here to manie considering how God hath blessed this land with a great increase of people...

She urged that these kind of people be sent forth from the land. In January 1601, she repeated her advice in a Royal proclamation allowing a Lubeck merchant to take away such

> Negroes and blackamores which are carried into this realm, to the great annoyance of her own liege people (Walvin, 1973).

These are some of the earliest recorded comments about black people living in British cities and they appropriately set the scene for a historical dimension which provides a working framework for this chapter. We need to observe whether this hostility towards black people persisted in Britain and whether the role played by political leaders in this social phenomenon was perceived by black people as welcoming or hostile. The period after the second world war is often cited as the time when race relations and immigration played a significant role in British politics. However immigration was not a new phenomenon to Britain in the 1950s.

During the 18th century Irish people were encouraged to emigrate to England for the purpose of building roads, railways and canals. The underdevelopment of Ireland by England resulted in a large reserve labour force who, due the prevailing poverty in Ireland, were willing to emigrate to pursue employment. In the late 19th century large number settled in England (see Rees, 1982). During the 1950s people from commonwealth countries came to Britain for the same reasons as the Irish immigrants. Under colonial rule, the British had systematically underdeveloped the Commonwealth countries. Indeed, recruiting teams travelled from Britain to parts of the Caribbean to lure workers to assist in the rebuilding of the British economy. Free market forces were allowed to prevail.

When the slump followed the boom, Britain's special relationship with Commonwealth countries, and her open door policy on immigration, was replaced by restrictive legislation. The justification for the Commonwealth immigration legislation was presented to the British public as the route through which white British working class jobs could be secured, and with them the working class welfare state and the British way of life. At first these sentiments were mainly expressed by right wingers. However support quickly spread as this sort of rhetoric and pressure from the restrictionist right fell on fertile ground. Resentment towards these new 'coloured' foreigners calling themselves 'British citizen', entering Britain as equals and stirring up trouble by taking jobs, was inevitable. The 1958 race riots in Notting Hill and Worthing finally prompted the government to take a serious overview of the developing situation. The government's response appears to some extent conflicting; for on the one hand, it introduced discriminating immigration legislation to control immigration from the 'coloured' Commonwealth. It was an action aimed at appeasing white British anxieties, acknowledging that the black people were the problem, while at the same time it attempted to appease black communities by setting about the general management of the issues by initiating urban aid and poverty programmes.

This ambiguity in the political response was reflected in all areas of social policy, with policy makers vacillating between the directions and purpose of social welfare intervention. Negative views were not confined to the political 'right'; the liberal 'left' also treated the issues of immigration as a problem which demanded a paternalistic, assimilationist approach. In general the political view was that the status quo could be sustained while a process of acculturation and assimilation was pursued. Since the 1950s a range of political approaches have been evident and each has significantly influenced the nature of welfare provisions, including education services. I will briefly outline some of these phases and their impact on the British education system. Notions of assimilation and integration advocated the minimising of difference between cultures and races seeking to bind individuals together as human beings with as little conflict as possible. Roy Jenkins' (1966) definition of integration highlighted the core of this apparently unrealistic, naive and ill-conceived notion. According to the then Labour Home Secretary, education should aim to provide 'not a flattening process of assimilation but equal opportunity accompanied by cultural diversity, in an atmosphere of mutual tolerance'.

Education services reflect this ideology with their unwillingness to acknowledge the role and impact of the 'differences' of each ethnic group. For example, by refusing to examine Caribbean languages as units in their own rights, educators treated all black Commonwealth immigrants as if they were one homogeneous group. Cultural pluralism encouraged an understanding, recognition and respect for ethnic groups, with an appreciation of the role of diversities. This thinking led to a 'special needs' approach in education emphasising the areas of the black child's education which demanded extra resources.

Multiculturalism grew from the cultural pluralist approach in that it encouraged white pupils and teachers to learn about and respect different cultural practices of other ethnic groups. Ahmed et al (1986) summarises these exhortations as the three S's, the sari, samosa and steel band. She examines why they played an important role in school curriculum. 'Cultural relativism,' the tendency to assume that all cultures are equally valid and therefore members of one culture have no right to criticise members of another culture by using their own standards of judgement' (see Channer and Parton, 1990), was in vogue at this time and is now only tentatively loosening its grip to permit an anti-racist ideology to pervade the education services.

These periods of social and political experimentation undoubtedly influenced the nature and pace of government intervention into areas of state provision such as education. The studies discussed in this chapter can be dated by the issues they choose to consider as central to their research.

There have been a number of shifts in emphasis in this long running debate. However, whatever the social and political complexion, the concept of 'underachievement' has remained central in the past thirty years. A number of researchers question the extent to which the concept of underachievement can be said to be foolproof, some challenge methodological approaches and consequently the findings of studies that hold to this notion. Others (Wright, 1988; Gillborn, 1990) suggest that this term is counter-productive as it could be see to locate the problem within the individual pupil while ignoring organisational factors. Wright states:

> The nature of the education experience of black students, especially those of Afro-Caribbean origin, may be better understood in terms of 'educational disadvantage' or 'inequality' rather than in terms of 'underachievement'. In advancing this type of analysis, we are drawing attention to the structural and institutional realities within which the situation of the black student within the education system needs to be understood (Wright, 1988, p.126).

Figueroa (1991) notes that statements about 'underachievement of black children are misleading and are part and parcel of the social construction of 'race'. He regards them as myths which are constantly sustained through social arrangements, process, behaviour and discourse. He states:

> ... the crux of the matter is that the educational system has often not met the educational needs of the black ethnic minority children... and indeed has actually worked to the disadvantage of these children. (p.156)

The present book will continue to utilise the concept of 'underachievement', because it is firmly rooted in the literature and operates as an essential frame of reference in much of the debate.

Summary of a range of studies

During the 1960-1980s, studies which examined the educational attainment rates of children from the Caribbean generally concluded that these children were not performing as well as white indigenous children (Tomlinson, 1983, p.28). A range of studies undertaken during this time undoubtedly reflects the wider socio-political debate discussed above. A number of authors, (Tomlinson, 1983, Wright, 1988) have summarised the findings of several of these studies completed in the last twenty years. Others have undertaken evaluations of many of these studies. Taylor (1981) conducted a critical evaluation of the methodologies of research concerning children of Caribbean descent. Troyna (1984) challenges the notion of 'underachievement', its conceptual framework and assumptions in the current debate. He also critically examines the ways in which evidence for black underachievement has been generated and presented. Drew and Gray's study (1990) purports to undermine much of the research which concerns itself with black pupils' attainment in British schools. They too question the methodologies, sample sizes and findings of these studies, which have resulted in what Troyna (1984) describes as a misguided use of 'benevolent multiculturalism'.

A number of other researchers regard these studies as lacking in credibility because of the small samples used. However, criticisms of inadequate sample size is not supported by Tomlinson (1983). Indeed she notes that many of the studies use total samples of over 600 children.

Whilst refuting the criticisms about sample sizes, she highlights two major concerns with the pre-eighties studies. Firstly, a number of small scale studies have been extensively quoted and have therefore been given undue importance. Secondly, she points out that a number of the large scale studies were completed during a period when a number of the black children in the school system were correctly called 'immigrants'. Factors which applied to that group may not currently hold equal significance for black British born children. Despite these criticisms the results of the earliest studies still pervade much of the current debate on black children's school experience.

Education researchers have made various and different approaches to investigations into the academic attainment and experiences of black children in British schools. Psychometric tests which measure ability potential or intelligence via standard IQ verbal and non-verbal tests were used during this period as one form of measurement (Houghton, 1966; Payne, 1969; Bhatnager, 1970; Griffiths, 1982). Studies using standardised group tests of attainment in English, reading and maths were yet another point of reference (Little, 1975; Mabey, 1981). Exploration into the use and misuse of special need provision (Coard, 1971; Tomlinson, 1981) provided further insights into this debate. Researchers such as Driver (1977), Swann (1985) and more recently Drew and Grey (1989) have examined black pupils' attainment in school-leaving qualifications. The factors cited in these studies as 'explaining' the poor academic performance of black children of Caribbean parents are relevant here. Wright (1988) separates these factors into three categories: firstly, psychogenic factors such as ability, motivation and self-esteem. Secondly, she locates studies which focus on sociogenic issues, for example, home background and occupational status of parents. The third category are the studies which explore aspects of school experience such as teacher expectation and pupil-teacher relationships.

Psychogenic factors

Challenging a growing environmental approach to the debate on the educational underachievement of black children, Jensen (1969) and Eysenck (1971) made a number of assertions. They claimed that IQ tests measured something real and significant called intelligence. They found that the results of their research correlated highly with success in school and later life. Consequently they suggested that compensatory education programmes in the USA. designed to raise the IQ of 'disadvantaged children' had failed to produce significant results because 80% of the IQ differences between individuals are genetic in origin and only 20% are caused by environmental factors. These researchers claimed that their research findings indicated that, on average, American black children scored fifteen points below white children in IQ tests and there are strong indications that this difference is genetically determined.

This level of technical rationality which ignores the reality of various reference points, has been strongly contested for a number of years. Swann (1985) particularly in the case of West Indians disputes it, and our own investigations leave us in no doubt that IQ is not a significant factor in underachievement.

Low self-esteem was also cited as central to the underachievement of children of Caribbean parentage. Coard (1971), Milner (1975) and Mabey (1981) found that these children lacked confidence in their academic abilities. Although this notion was popular during the 1960s and 1970s and ultimately had a strong influence on the development of multicultural education philosophies, a number of educationalists questioned findings which claimed a strong relationship between low self-esteem and poor academic achievement. Macintosh et al (1985 p.141) notes that even if scholastic performances were very much clearer than they are, we could still not assert that low self-esteem had been shown to be the cause of poor performance. They observed that a child who, for whatever reason, is doing badly at school may well be inclined to agree with such statements as 'I'm doing as well in school as I would like to' or 'I often feel discouraged at school'. These are two of the items to be found in the most widely used self- esteem inventory.

Stone (1981) elaborates on significant issues and argues that :

through political, social, literary and musical styles, people create alternative sources of selfhood. We should not therefore be surprised to find a normal or average distribution of self-concept scores amongst black children in Britain. (p. 236)

Sociogenic explanations

Some researchers have taken a functionalist or positivist approach, exploring reasons such as migration, separation, reconstituted families, social deprivation, socio-economic factors and social class as 'reasons' for the underachievement of black children. I will examine a number of these explanations.

Migration

The view that the academic underachievement of children from the Caribbean is related to migration has been formally and informally expressed. It implies that many of these children were separated for long periods from their parents, who came to England leaving them with relatives in the Caribbean. And once they arrived in England these children had to come to terms with a new home, a strange country, the change in climate, the transition for some from a rural to an urban society, the disorienting effect of being plunged into a new cultural milieu as well as the likelihood of encountering new siblings. Such a range of new experiences over a short time could be, at best, stressful and at worst, traumatic. In regard to education, therefore, these children were said to be facing additional problems which may have hindered their progress in school (see Houghton, 1966, Driver, 1977).

Given that immigration from the Caribbean came to a standstill in the 1960s this factor has little weight in the current debate. However there appears to be a fundamental disagreement about the experiences of children of Caribbean parents who were born in Britain or experienced little or no schooling in the Caribbean. McEwan et al (1975) argued that their research findings indicated that children born in Britain performed better that the 'immigrant' children. However Essen and Ghodsian (1979) concluded that 'poorer school performance' is generally found among 'first generation' immigrants but children of West Indian origin still do rather worse at 'second generation' level. Johns (1986) records the felt experiences of many pupils who received some of their schooling in the

Caribbean. They recall that their level of academic attainment was at least a year in advance of their peers in British schools. As a result they recollect being bewildered by the retrogressive step they were asked to take and the possible effect this may have had on their subsequent school career. The life history respondents in this study who had experienced some schooling in the Caribbean agreed with Johns (1986) — indeed one suggested that 'it was after we slowed down we could get on with the hidden agenda of underachieving'.

Socio-economic factors

Influenced by economic and social surveys such as those undertaken by the Community Relations Commission (1974) and the PEP (1977), education policy makers were led to conclude that, generally speaking, children from Caribbean families came from severely disadvantaged home conditions and would therefore, alongside white working class children, demonstrate academic under-performance.

Most recent figures show that the majority of black families are concentrated in areas of poor housing. In addition they show that 88% of a national sample of minorities lived in pre-1939 dwellings, compared with 48% of the white population, and that 30% of 'West Indians' shared their dwellings compared to 3.8% of whites. Reports also showed that 34% of 'West Indians' lived in conditions of two or more people per bedroom compared with only 11% of whites. Employment figures also points to ethnic minority men, particularly 'West Indians' tending to have low status jobs, earn less, and suffer more unemployment.

> The immigrant population suffer from working in low paid industries at low pay. Whereas 40% of the whites in employment are in professional managerial or white collar jobs, only 8% of the 'West Indian' men, 8% of the Pakistanis/Bangladeshis, 20% of the Indian and 30% of the East African are employed in such work. The remainder of the ethnic minority workers are in semi-skilled or unskilled manual work with a medium gross income (depending on the country of origin) of between four to six pounds less than the national medium gross wage (PEP, 1977).

Thus the DES has tended to assume that 'West Indian' underachievement in schools is due to the same social disadvantages as affect underprivileged white children. As a result, no particular strategy to combat the problem of 'West Indian' children has been pursued. The concept of 'educational disadvantage' was first expressed in the Plowden Report (1976), which argued that black children and white from the inner city areas were equally deprived. In essence therefore, the then Department of Education and Science (DES) had assumed that by tackling the problems caused by poverty collectively, the low performance of all children, including 'West Indians', would be alleviated. If social and economic disadvantages were the only cause of low academic achievement as supposed by the DES, then one would expect 'West Indian' and white children from the same catchment area to score similar results in tests. However, evidence from studies carried out in 'education priority areas' (EPA) demonstrated that underprivileged white children were performing at a higher level than pupils of Caribbean origin. It is clear, therefore, that the special problems and needs of 'West Indian' children are not a mere extension of the problems of the white disadvantaged. More than twenty years after the outset of the debate Swann (1985) discovered that the black pupil's position had not altered significantly. 'West Indian origin children obtained very poor examination success rates, compared to Asian and white children. In an attempt to explain the lower level of conceptual development of children from the Caribbean, Griffiths (1982) offered the notion of multiple deprivation and the single-parent family situation as core factors which negatively influenced the results achieved by these black children. On arrival in Britain most individuals from the Caribbean were compelled to accept low status occupations regardless of their previous professional qualifications or experiences.

Whilst racism still pervades British employment, notions that all black families are working class or even members of the underclass ignore the growing numbers of black professionals who are contributing a great deal to society in economic and educational terms. (*Women's Journal*, 1987, Phoenix 1988).

Although research findings support the arguments that the black population share certain socio-economic characteristics with the white unskilled worker, there is also evidence to suggest that there are differences between the two groups in their attitude towards education. Caribbean parents are known to have a high regard for education per se as well as the benefits it brings (Stone, 1981; Tomlinson, 1983). In the area of education, recent white working class communities appear to lack the wherewithal to engage the tradition of self-help and community organisation evidenced by the Chartists. On the other hand black communities have galvanised themselves into action and sought to improve the education services offered to their own children (see Johns, 1986). The West Indian community has undertaken several initiatives with regard to their children's education both locally and nationally. Exemplars are the Redbridge Study (1978) conducted by parents, the pressures exerted by the West Indian parents in Hackney to force the schools to teach their children more effectively (see Venning, 1983), and the growth of supplementary schools around the country. These initiatives clearly demonstrate an attempt on the part of African-Caribbean parents to improve their children's educational attainment (Chevannes, 1982). With regard to education black families appear to share the values held by white middle class parents. Some researchers (Bristol, 1986) demonstrate some correlation between the educational achievement of these pupils and their mother's social class and economic status.

The reliance on poverty alone as an explanation for the poor performance of black children in British schools is inadequate. Swann (1985) concludes that:

> school performance has long been known to show a close correlation with socio-economic status and social class, in the case of all children. The ethnic minorities, however, are particularly disadvantaged in social terms and there can no longer be any doubt that this extra deprivation is the result of racial prejudice and discrimination, especially in the areas of employment and housing.

School experience: teacher-pupil interactions

Swann (1985) also comments on the contribution teacher's attitudes make to the black child's school experience. The committee believed that only a very small minority of teachers could be said to be racist in the commonly accepted sense. However it stated that a teacher's attitude towards and expectations of black pupils may be subconsciously influenced by negative stereotypes or patronising views of their abilities and potential. These views may prove to be self-fulfilling prophecies, with pupils responding to situations according to their labels. This can be seen as a form of 'unintentional racism'.

A number of studies examine teacher pupil interactionsand some explore other aspects of school experiences. Both Brittan (1976) and Giles (1977) noted how the teachers in their studies perceived African-Caribbean children to be of low ability and to have behavioural problems. Further evidence on teachers' perceptions of 'West Indian' children in relation to other racial groups was furnished by the study of Rex and Tomlinson (1979). Some of the views expressed by head teachers interviewed in the study were as follows: 'They (West Indians) are bound to be slower, it's their personalities, they lack concentration' and 'West Indian children are boisterous and less keen on education than Asians. This is known obviously' (Rex and Tomlinson, 1979).

Suggestions by the Redbridge (1978) report that negative stereotypes and expectations might be a causative factor in 'West Indian' underperformance was greeted with piety and defensiveness by local representatives of the teachers' unions. The chairman of Redbridge education committee commented:

> 'In general terms, and I mean this in the nicest possible way, the 'West Indian' are more interested in the creative activities, in sports, ...Do you want a hard working, high achieving young man or woman, or do you want to develop their present happy approach and make things up in due course?' (quoted in Jeffcoate, 1979).

This is a most disturbing statement, all the more so, given the status of the author. He appears to be oblivious of how his views might impact on the children in his care.

A number of studies examine at great length teacher-pupil interactions and aim to explain how the teacher can influence the educational performance of an African-Caribbean child in school. In an ethnographic study in the West Midlands, Driver (1979) questioned the accuracy of teachers' perceptions of the African-Caribbean child's behaviour, unlike Middleton (1983) who had not challenged teachers' views on the matter but had concluded: 'It is not denied in this study that the black boy is clearly more demanding, or badly behaved than his white counterpart' (p.117). Through the concept of 'cultural competence' and 'confusion' Driver outlined the difficulties teachers faced when attempting to interpret the behaviour of black pupils (see Driver, 1977). Both Driver and Wright (1988) found evidence to support the view that the teacher allowed the difficulties of the pupils' social behaviour in the classroom situation to become institutionalised by allowing this to influence their decisions when they assessed these pupils. However, Wright challenges Driver's notion of 'confusion' as a significant element in this debate. She comments that:

> it is difficult to accept 'confusion' as a sufficient cause for misallocation in banding and setting. How, for example, is it possible to confuse a mark of 82% in allocating a child to a CSE set? And how is it possible to 'confuse' an internal report which gives an assessment score of 6...indicating that all subjects were graded A or B — and still allocate the child to the bottom of three bands? (Wright, 1985b, p.22.)

Although criticised for its inflexibility and inability to take account of non-verbal communications, Green's (1983, 1985) study, which collected data via the Flanders Schedule (1970), provides data which largely supports Wright's conclusions. He noted that in general white and Asian children benefit substantially from more teacher attention in the classroom than children of African-Caribbean origin, whatever the tolerance level of the teacher.

A number or ethnographic studies have used interviews with black children and young people in an attempt to discover their response to the negative experiences outlined above. A significant proportion of these pupils expressed frustration, anger and disenchantment with the poor relationships they encountered.

In their qualitative studies both Wright (1988) and Gillborn (1990) found that a number of black pupils responded overtly to what they deemed to be unreasonable amounts of criticism. Gillborn catalogues elements of the teacher-pupil relationship which appear to threaten many white teachers and result in an excessive level of criticism of black pupils. Teachers' negative responses to styles of walking and the use of patois were on occasions a catalyst for such behaviour patterns being used as a strategy of resistance Gillborn (1990). Gillborn also identifies a group of pupils — as illustrated by 'Paul Dixon' — who 'kept a low profile', minimising the amount and nature of conflict situations by choosing to adapt and accommodate rather than confront.

Creole in the classroom

Among the behaviours seen as emphasising black pupil's ethnicity and which appeared to threaten white teachers, Gillborn cites black pupils' use of Creole in conversation. Wright's (1985:a) interview with a white deputy headteacher highlights the extent to which the use of a foreign language can create resentment:

> We've got a problem at the moment, which is very nasty.. we are being faced with a barrage of patois. It is so worrying because you see when that happens we as teachers have a choice. We either ignore it, but if it is done in public you feel threatened, or you feel you are showing weakness if you just ignore it. You can either react equally aggressively and verbally in Spanish or French, which in fact is what is happening but that is not helpful, or as one member of staff said to me today, I came close to clobbering him today (1985a p.13).

Interviews with black pupils provides further evidence which demonstrates that pupils' use of Creole was not always as a form of overt resistance, but that to some it was an integral element in their cultural make-up (see Mac an Ghaill, 1988). This sense of pride in an aspect of one's culture has to some extent been validated by research findings that demonstrate how Caribbean Creoles used in Britain have changed and adapted, reflecting the importance of language as a dynamic part of a culture.

Creole, language or dialect

It would be misleading to suggest that all sectors of the African-Caribbean community would lobby for Creole to be acknowledged as a language in its own right. Many Caribbeans living in Britain as well as those living in their home countries maintain a strong ambivalence towards Creole. This is due to generations of socio-linguistic conditioning which has persuaded many people that certain ways of speaking are associated with poverty, lack of education and cultural limitation, while other styles of speech are associated with social, educational and material success.

Despite the ambivalence and hostility to Creole, the debate with regard to its status as a dialect or language appears to have been reliably settled. Edwards states that:

> In terms of its systems of meaning, rules of grammar and capacity as a medium of communication, Creole has all the characteristics of a fully developed language (Edwards, 1979).

Central to the discussion of the status of Creole is the consideration of its power to interfere in the black child's learning patterns. Both Rampton (1981) and Swann (1985) were conclusive on the concept of interference. They state that, for the majority of West Indian children in our schools who were born and brought up in this country, linguistic factors play no part in underachievement (Swann, 1985) Gibson (1986). But ethnographic research refutes this bold statement, with examples of such children who experienced difficulties of comprehension during their schooling. Formal research (Edwards, 1979) and informal discussions (Jamdaigni et al, 1982) outline the serious impact of the emphasis on 'Standard' English on black children's educational performance. However, there appears to be little political will to address an issue which can be explained away as carelessness in written work.

Studies which locate 'achievers'

A number of studies attempt to specify factors associated with academic success. Many of these research projects have been undertaken in the 1980s and foster a subject centred approach.

Driver's study received a great deal of attention when he claimed to show 'How West Indian pupils do better (than white pupils) at school' (1980). His work alleged that these pupils were not underachieving to the level suggested by previous studies. These assertions found little support in the field of education. Indeed, both his methodology and findings have been severely criticised. Taylor (1981) found that the nature of Driver's data did not entitle him to draw the educational conclusions that he arrived at. Nevertheless his work has drawn attention to the fact that the 'underachieving' label does not belong to all pupils of African-Caribbean origin.

Further studies (Sharpe, 1976; Fuller, 1980) have supported Driver's assertions concerning the gender differential in academic performance and have highlighted the fact that, whilst studies in the 1980s unanimously supported the notion of underachievement, a number of them had also made similar observations (see Houghton, 1966; Little, Mabey and Witaker, 1968; Payne, 1969). In seeking to explain his findings Driver suggested that the matrifocal nature of the Caribbean family was an influencing factor. The girls' results, he asserts,

> appeared to be due in part to the strongly held viewpoint of the West Indian mother, in particular, that their daughters must be seen as the social mainstay of their family's future (Driver, 1977).

Some writers find Driver's opinions about the nature of the Caribbean family historically dubious (e.g. Chigwada, 1987). Although such statements may not intentionally seek to pathologise black communities, a focus which is concerned with how subcultural values and attitudes may be linked to educational performance is likely to be seen as 'adopting a discourse of deficit. The main social images constructed by this approach portray the black community as a problem' (Mac an Ghaill, 1988). Others have cited other reasons for his findings that the girls do well. Parental (both mother and father) support, apprehension about leaving school and a positive attitude to being female figured strongly in the research findings of Sharpe (1976), Fuller (1980) and Chigwada (1987). They found that black school girls were aware that education, employment and economic security would provide them with a lever to fight a social system that often relegates black people to the lowest social rung. However, when unpicking school experiences and classroom interaction, these researchers found that in general these academically achieving girls were unwilling to play the role of 'a good pupil'. They certainly rejected the racist curriculum and resented racist staff members but they highly valued the acquisition of academic qualifications. Chigwada (1987) describes their position as 'anti-school but pro-education.'

> The Brent girls did not conform to the white stereotype of 'high achiever'. They were often in conflict with teachers over rules they considered 'trivial', arrived late for lessons, read magazines in the class, openly contested the teacher's authority. Such behaviour was calculated to irritate teachers and present an image of not caring...yet they all completed set work on time (Chigwada, 1987 p. 1).

To some extent these girls appeared to be using a different approach those pupils epitomised by Gillborn's Paul Dixon (1990), who chose to keep a low profile, be non-confrontational and suppress any characteristics of ethnicity which might threaten teachers. Both Fuller and Gillborn agree that it is unhelpful to present a polarised debate around conformity and deviance. It becomes only too easy to assume that academic striving and achievement need to be synonymous with subscribing and conforming to popular and dominant values upheld by the school, and to see school failure as necessarily indicative of rejection of those same values. For black pupils who seek academic success in a racially hostile school environment, deviance could be a well-measured stance which permits self-esteem to remain in tact while students aim to secure a educational foundation for their future.

Research, the black community and the role of this project

In common with much of the research of its time, Bagley, Bart and Wong (1978) cited psychogenic, sociogenic and socio-linguistic factors as influential areas which determined academic success for black children. This, and other studies like it, which claim to redress the pathological trend in the underachievement debate, have caused concern among members of the African-Caribbean community (Phoenix, 1988.) Rather than reversing the trend, the authors seem to be underscoring and confirming the pathological stance. They state:

> The authoritarianism which is a traditional feature of child- rearing in Jamaican parents (Phillips, 1973) may have been functional in an era when non-conformity and creativity were heavily sanctioned. Keeping children in their place was, perhaps, a cultural lag from the days of slavery into an era of domination by a white or light-coloured minority in Jamaica. Today such parental values are no longer functional and indeed create considerable problems when black teenagers, influenced by the standards of their white peers, may in consequence rebel at the strictness and passive conservatism of their parents as they reorient themselves into ideological positions which are highly critical of English society (p.16).

In the above quote and elsewhere in their study Bagley *et.al.* excel in proffering negative stereotypes and pathological images of a community. They present a view of a group of people who are unable to adapt their approach to an outdated discipline even after the passage of time and who are unquestionably content to accept injustice and unjustified oppression for themselves and their children. The writers appear unable to explain why Jamaicans but no other islanders should suffer from this 'cultural-lag'.

Images of a purposeless, dictatorial regime requires evaluation, yet they appear to ignore the weight of responsibility carried by black parents in a society which denies their children basic rights and interprets their behaviour in an unfavourable light. The high numbers of disproportionately black children in the care system, and of black youths and adults in mental institutions and receiving custodial sentences highlights the extent to which racism impacts on the black family in Britain, rather than the extent to which black youths are rebelling from their families' standards (Liverpool, 1986). Indeed this study registers the gratitude of black adults to these 'strict parents' for their commitment, often at great emotional and financial sacrifice, to ensuring that their children were protected from the consequences of succumbing to the traps and pitfalls of a racist society.

The black communities' bewilderment at the process and consequence of 'being researched ad nauseam' has been recorded by a number of black social scientists (Ahmed *et.al.*, 1986, Lashley, 1986). Black respondents at the receiving end of this experience have also openly registered their ambivalence towards the wisdom of this exercise.

> Judith: In a way, you see our lives as worse than we do because you have an alternative to measure it against. But in another way it's worse for us because you can go on with your life. Tomorrow you can leave Kilby and go to your white areas. But we are always black living in a racist society. You can't really know what it's like for a black woman. That's why I think that although what you have done is good, I think that black women should carry out their own studies (Mac an Ghaill, 1988. p. 187).

Mac an Ghaill (1988) acknowledges the possible impact of racism and sexism on his research. He also refers to other researchers (Meyenn, 1979, Lawrence, 1981) who found that subjects did not share certain areas of their private lives with researchers when inequality of power was central to the relationship (eg black female subjects and white male researchers).

A fuller discussion concerning the ethical and political problems which arise in social science follows in Chapter 3 on methodology, with a view to addressing Matza's (1969) view of the role and responsibility of social research. He notes that:

> A serious commitment to the subjective view cannot grudgingly stop with the appreciation of the subject's definition of his (sic) specific deviant predicament. It must also entail an appreciation of the ordinary subject's philosophical definition of his general predicament. Concretely, this means that the capacity to intend must be treated seriously and occupy a central place in the analysis on social life (p.25).

As a member of the African-Caribbean community I regard the recent subject centred research projects as progressive. However it appears that certain aspects of the community's life are neglected due to research relationships where subjects are conscious of the potential for racism and secularism. Being aware of these research barriers may discourage subjects from sharing in sensitive discussion about their life experiences. Mac an Ghaill (1989) notes that a number of his subjects attended church, (p.117). Other researchers have also noted the religious nature of the African-Caribbean family (Fitzherbert, 1968; see Liverpool, 1986), although (Tomlinson, 1983) to date no detailed evaluation of this aspect of their lives in relation to academic achievement has been undertaken. Could it be that the role religion plays in the individual and communal lives of the African community is a sensitive and delicate area which requires the integral element of trust in the research relationship?

The following chapter presents factual information about religious sects which are popularly attended by African-Caribbeans in Britain. A wider discussion about the role such sects may play in the social mobility of their members will be undertaken within the framework of the sociology of religion and the sociology of sects.

Chapter 2

Race, Religion and Social Action

In Chapter one I outlined the role racism has played and continues to play in the educational experiences of African-Caribbean children in British schools. The combination of a range of factors were identified as 'causing' the poor academic results of African-Caribbean children. Undermining a child's self-esteem was one significant psychogenic factor and there were many sociogenic factors such as unemployment and poor housing. Friction in the relationships between black children and their white teachers was identified by researchers (Gillborn, 1990, Mac an Ghaill, 1989) as widespread and the core reason for the academic underachievement of many black pupils.

The process and impact of migration has been cited (Houghton, 1966) as having some detrimental impact on the educational experience of children from the Caribbean. Chapter one points out that since immigration from the Caribbean came to standstill in the 1960s this can hold little weight as a factor in the current education debate. However the impact of racism felt by African-Caribbeans who came to England during the 50s and 60s caused bewilderment at the time and has had long-term effects. Chapter one also noted the differing socio-political responses to the presence of a black British population. The newcomers had not expected such hostility from the 'host' community.

This chapter presents a vivid description of the reception experienced by black newcomers to England in the 1950s and 1960s, based on pieces of research which rest largely on personal quotations from individuals who were at the receiving end of these experiences. The chapter sets out a relevant context for further discussion. The culture shock and rejection faced by these individuals and other members of their communities created a sense of meaningfulness, leaving them to seek the refuge of religion as a 'shield against a meaningless society'. Rejected by white mainstream churches African-Caribbeans set up their own self-sufficient religious organisations. Example of these sects are discussed in this chapter.

An exploration of the experiences of Caribbeans who came to Britain in the 1950s is presented in Dodgson's (1984) *Motherland.* By using a similar conversational approach to the research method used in this book, Dodgson reveals the extent to which rejection and oppression was an undisputed fact of life for the new black immigrants. I make particular use of the quotations she presents in her work to substantiate the historic issues presented elsewhere. Quotations also come from a workshop session (1990) where black Christian women met to discuss their early years in England (Channer and Channer, 1990).

Arriving in Britain

Fryer (1984) describes the immigrants thus:

> The great majority of West Indian settlers were in their twenties and they had plenty to offer Britain. Most white people in this country believed and many still suppose that the bulk of them were unskilled manual workers. But that is not so. Of the men who came here, a mere 13 per cent had no skills; of the women, only 5 per cent. In fact, one in four of the men, and half of the women were non-manual workers. Almost half of the men (46 per cent) and over a quarter of the women (27 per cent) were skilled manual workers (p.374).

Many studies of West Indian emigration to Britain have described a variety of 'push' factors which caused West Indians to leave their islands and 'pull' factors which attracted them to England. 'Push' factors, stemmed from the underdeveloped state of the economy — a situation which is directly attributed to the area's colonial relationship with Britain. The 'pull' factors were derived from the economic boom in post-war Britain which provided many job vacancies. At first British industry gladly absorbed the trickle of 'West Indian' workers into Britain.

The newcomers took their British citizenship seriously and regarded themselves not as strangers but as English people. Their ideas about Britain were largely derived from their colonial education. They were brought up to respect the English way of life and hoped to live and work in Britain as equals. They knew about British history, the Queen, the Constitution and had been led to believe that they would be welcomed. Dodgson's (1984) subjects spoke of how surprised they were to discover that English people knew little, if anything, about them.

> The comments and questions of the English people they met were irritating and sometimes offensive. Some genuinely believed that West Indians had lived in trees or worn only pieces of cloth around their waist at home. Even those who were less ignorant could not distinguish between West Indians and West Africans. They were asked questions which clearly showed that they did not know where the islands of the West Indies were located (eg Is British Guiana the same as Ghana?) nor did they realise that, for most, English was their first language (eg How did you manage to learn English so quickly?) (p.49).

The notion of 'white racial superiority' was obvious in all aspects of British life. The newcomers soon found out that even if industry welcomed them, socially they were outcasts. Instances of rejection and refusals at hotels, pubs, dance halls and restaurants were widely reported. Many West Indians who came during the 50s and 60s describe the pain and tension they felt because of the racial prejudice they encountered.

One of Dodgson's subjects said,

> I was amazed that people actually didn't know anything about the West Indies and we all knew about them. First you feel angry and then I think it's a survival thing and you start to feel sorry for them. I remember once on the street someone asked me where I put my tail. The person was serious. I looked at him and said 'the same place where you keep yours'.

Another said,

> I stopped thinking about Britain as the mother country in the first year, in the first months... the sense of belonging is not there (Dodgson, pp.52, 53).

The hostility, oppression and racial abuse that regularly occurred in public places prompted the immigrants to 'keep to themselves'. With reasonable living and working conditions many might have found some sense of refuge in this hostile environment. But even basic necessities such as housing, employment and child care facilities were denied them. Despite their skills, the newcomers found in most cases, that they had to settle for a lower status job than they had enjoyed at home.

Conditions of work were generally unattractive with low pay, long and often unsocial hours and poor prospects. Few found clerical jobs and work as shop assistants. Employers felt that 'the public might not like it'. Even when seeking training as nurses, the newcomers where discouraged from taking the State Registered Nurse examination, which allowed them opportunity for promotion. Instead the State Enrolled Nursing qualification, a shorter course with lower status, was offered to them. Mrs B (Channer and Channer, 1990) said,

> A lot of us fell for that [doing the SEN instead of SRN]. If we were given the chance at the time to sit the test to do SRN a lot of us would have got through. We were sort of cheap labour really.

The newcomers identified and experienced racial discrimination in the feelings of personal dislike or uneasiness which was directed against them by other individuals. Rules, conventions and traditions of various institutions also operated against them. Sharing these unpleasant experiences with family members in the Caribbean was not always an option. When training to become a nurse, Mrs B (Channer and Channer, 1990) found that:

> ... the black girls used to get very low marks. I never used to write home and tell my Dad. Oh no, I wouldn't do that because he'd be worried out of his mind. No, I always tell him I'm happy.

She also said

> I went to a hospital in Manchester, as an auxiliary. Some of the patients don't want you to come near, they don't want you to touch them. It makes you feel bitter but you want the job so you have to stick to it. If you tell them anything they will complain to the matron and you will get the sack.

Most of the new arrivals found it extremely difficult to find accommodation when they arrived in Britain. West Indian migrants did not qualify for council houses and no special provision was made to enable the Caribbeans to find accommodation. In the private market there was a general unwillingness among white landlords to take black tenants. The humiliation felt when doors were slammed shut in their face was only one example of the impact of racism. There were often restrictions such as ten o' clock evening curfew, restricted visiting, extra charges for the use of lighting and heating; others were refused the use of some electrical appliances. In many houses children were not allowed. If a woman was found to be pregnant she was often evicted.

Mrs E said,

> I was looking for a better reception towards us. I wouldn't have left Jamaica if I'd known. I lost days from work looking for a room. The situation was very bad. I felt bitter.

Another said,

> Them rent you a room, but you can't do anything. Sometimes you had to hide to iron. There's certain times I had to wake up about five o'clock and I do a little ironing. That time the children were small and I wasn't going to work... but no light... no light during the whole day. No visitors, nobody can come look for you (Channer and Channer, 1990).

One interviewee who had been evicted said,

> When we gone to work and come back everything was thrown out. Everything that we possess was outside... outside on the ground. We can't get back in. And in those days we can't go to the police (Dodgson, 1984, p.29).

Arranging care for children when both parents were out at work was expensive and often highly unsatisfactory. Parents had good cause to worry about the motivation and childcare skills of certain childminders. One woman interviewed by Dodgson said,

> A woman said to me one day, 'What a lively baby, oh she's nice and sweet. where do you take her?' I told her and she said, 'Lord have mercy, you mustn't take your baby down there 'cause she puts them downstairs on the basement floor.' So I went down to the basement, I pushed past the woman and I looked at all the pickney on the floor that had been brought there in the morning time (p.40).

The prospects of securing a better future for their children had been a significant factor in the decision to leave the Caribbean. Parents were heart-broken at the ill-treatment and abuse of their children at the hands of expensive childminders and other social institutions.

Each area of the newcomer's life was besieged with problems. Their presence was resented. Each encounter with white people bought new hazards. They suffered racial abuse, insults, indignities, 'colour tax', the 'colour bar' and ultimately race riots in which black people were murdered. As noted in Chapter one, even the government legitimated and institutionalised racist policies. Disappointment and disillusionment were the essence of the Caribbean newcomer's life. Their expectations and aspiration had been dashed.

It is the knowledge of the level of emotional turmoil and personal frustration that engulfed these black people in Britain which gave rise to the idea of this book. Namely, if this group were to survive in such an emotionally destructive environment they would need some sort of refuge from the daily social and psychological onslaught. From personal observation of the African-Caribbean community it appeared that religion provided such a refuge, since many of them appeared to value many aspects of their religious affiliation. Although it is difficult to evaluate 'subjective' factors such as 'value of religious adherence', try in the early part of the book to set the scene for the study by exploring the role of religion in the experience of African-Caribbeans in Britain, drawing on some of the research literature in the field.

Hill (1970) states that religion is of great significance for Caribbeans in that it is often inseparable from the socio-cultural aspects of behaviour.

On average 69% of the British Caribbean population attended regularly one or other of the six major branches of the Christian church. After leaving their home countries this pattern of church attendance has altered remarkably.

Hill (1970) states,

> Clearly some major variables have been injected into the situation to disturb what we should otherwise have expected to be the normal pattern of behaviour (pp.37, 38).

Besides the social expectations discussed above, those who came from Caribbean countries had certain expectations about British religion.

Hill (1970) continues,

> The West Indian comes from a predominantly English cultural background in which most of his major social institutions are based upon English ideal types. Probably the most outstanding example of this is religion. All the major branches of the Western church are firmly established in the West Indies, and their pattern of worship as well as their beliefs and practices are very largely identical with those found in similar churches in this country (p.41).

For African-Caribbeans coming to England in the 1950s and 1960s a sense of disorientation was not surprising as they had left cohesive rural societies. They were launched into modern, complex urban societies which were fragmented by advanced technology and individualisation. Beyond this radical change of environment the new arrivals had to come to terms with dashed expectations and aspirations. Hill (1970) refers to the culture shock, disappointment and disillusionment that led to 'West Indian experience of anomie'. In his examination of religion Weber (1965) states that religion met the psychological need of the socially deprived by providing an explanation which makes sense of experiences that might otherwise seem senseless or a denial of God's providence.

In his list of conditions in which humans feel life is 'senseless' Weber (1965) includes political and social servitude, suffering and misery. Given the political and social servitude, suffering and misery that the black newcomers experienced in the 1950s and 1960s it might be expected that religion would be sought as a refuge for them in their new home.

> It would seem reasonable to expect that the churches could provide, if not an open sesame into wider society, at least a reference group with which the incoming migrant could readily identify himself and in which he could find unconditional acceptance. One could expect the indigenous churches to be providing a matrix of integration which in time would lead to full assimilation and to similar acceptance in wider society (Hill, 1970, p.37).

This was not to be the experience of Black migrants from the Caribbean. The rejection experienced in employment, housing and other aspects of their lives was reflected in the churches' rejection of black Christians. Many African-Caribbeans of that generation tell of the dismay, bewilderment and pain they suffered at being turned away from 'God's house'. Hill (1970) noted that white working class apathy to religion did not significantly impact on 'West Indians'. Despite rejection by white Christians, black British citizens, formerly members of mainstream Christian church, maintained their interest in religion and set up their own organisations.

Black people's absence from white Christian organisations is symptomatic of the socio-cultural rejection they experienced. Hill (1970) comments:

> I believe that the West Indian rejection of the church in Britain is not merely or even primarily a rejection of their beliefs or their traditional religious affiliations, but is a symbol of their disillusionment with, and disassociation from, the society and its culture which has rejected them (p.38).

He further observes that the high growth rate of West Indian Pentecostalist Assemblies in Britain began in 1964, the same year as race relations became a political issue during the General Election of that year. Racism formed the core of the black community's sense of 'meaninglessness', consequently the population turned inwards making use of their limited material and cultural resources to build and maintain self-sufficient churches. (In a later chapter I will explore other views [eg Marxism] which regard religion as dysfunctional and divisive in an attempt to present a balanced view of this.)

Other writers (Niebuhr, 1929, Schwartz, 1972) have examined the role religion plays in the lives of groups who need to bring meaning to negative social experiences. Membership of small religious groups, often called sects, is sometimes seen as having positive correlation to negative social experiences. A number of the religious groups which have blossomed in the African-Caribbean British Society are often referred to as sects. There is a long-standing debate about the use of terminology in this field (Martin, 1962). The specific distinction between sects, denominations and churches continues to attract some controversy.

Wilson's (1969) use of the term sect follows a general usage and refers to the small religious group in which membership is voluntary and conditional upon some mark of merit, understanding the group's teachings, or experience of some personal religious ecstasy upon the basis of which association can arise.

The sect could be regarded as a clearly defined community, which is of a size which permits only a minimal range of diversity of conduct. Wilson observes:

> It seeks itself to rigidify a pattern of behaviour and to make coherent its structures. It contends actively against every other social context possible for its adherent, offering itself as an all embracing, divinely prescribed society. The sect is not only an ideological unit, it is, to a greater or lesser degree, a social unit. Seeking to enforce behaviour on those who accept belief, and seeking every occasion to draw the faithful apart from the rest of society and into the company of each other.

Yinger (1971) also observed that the sect tends to dominate a large part of the social and the ideological life of its members.

There follows an outline of some of the sects which attracted and continue to attract, large numbers of black Britons. I consider the extent to which these sects and their philosophies provided and continue to provide a meaningful existence for their black adherents. And the extent to which the sects can address themselves to the realities of being black in Britain. Given that the book is concerned with those African-Caribbeans who seek to succeed in terms of acceptable societal values, the possible influences and religious beliefs on social action (eg academic achievement) is central to the discussion.

Seventh-Day Adventist History

Seventh-Day Adventist churches would not regard themselves as solely black organisations. Nevertheless their British membership is currently approximately 70 per cent black. The Seventh-Day Adventists trace their origin to the Millerites of the 19th century. William Miller, a Baptist preacher, became convinced in 1831 that he had discovered the key to the apocalyptic passages in the Old and New Testaments. This sect has a consistent approach by which knowledge is passed on to its members. They have a pragmatic view to group study and the grasping of church doctrine placing great emphasis on the searching of the scriptures.

Seventh-Day Adventist Theology

At the crux of Adventist theology is the belief that Christ is in the Holy of holies, a heavenly sanctuary. This sanctuary has its physical example in the ancient Jewish system of sacrificial offerings. In this sanctuary Christ has a dual role:

1. pleading to God the father on behalf of mankind;
2 judging the dead from the beginning of our world.

This important theology leads the Adventist advocate to continually assess his/her motives and actions.

In the judgement the use made of every talent will be scrutinised. How have we employed the capital lent us in Heaven? Will the Lord at His coming receive His own usury? Have we used our time, our pen, our voice, our money, our influence? What have we done for Christ, in the person of the poor, the affected, the orphan, or the widow? God has made us the depositories of His Holy word; what have we done with the light and truth given us to make us wise unto salvation? No value is attached to a mere profession of faith in Christ; only the love which is shown by works is counted genuine. The work of preparation is an individual work. We are not saved in groups (Schwartz, 1970, p. 100).

The member's earthly life influences his/her eternal destination. Adventists order their life so that Christ can be pleased with them at the time of judgement.

Christ's dual role in the sanctuary is known as the investigative judgement; this investigative process establishes the theological grounds for Adventist ideology. An individual will experience stages of slipping.

These experiences should become less and less, every mis-deed should be confessed in order to move on to a higher spiritual plain. A converted person's religious experience would penetrate to the very core of the character. The emphasis on the heavenly court scene induces the believer to maintain a strict standard of conduct.

> Every man's work passes in review before God and is registered for faithfulness or unfaithfulness. Opposite each name in the books of heaven is entered with terrible exactness every wrong work, every selfish act, every unfilled duty, and every secret sin, with every artful dissembling. Heaven-sent warnings or reproofs neglected, wasted moments, unimproved opportunities, the influence exerted for good or for evil, with its far-reaching results, all are chronicled by the recording angel. The law of God is the standard by which the characters and the lives of men will be tested in the judgements (Schwartz, 1970).

Adventists stipulate that the world is divided into two forces, Satan's force and God's force, that the words and deeds of a follower of this sect should be allied to God's force, whilst at the same time analysing Satan's force in all its implications, be it social, political, economic or religious.

Seventh-Day Adventist Ideology

Schwartz (1970) links Adventism to Weber's (1965) Protestants. They assume that the saved are placed on earth to labour in ways that are pleasing to God. Emphasising human volition and moral responsibility. Adventists should be righteous not wicked, they should be temperate rather than indulgent, they should have self-control rather than be spontaneous. Embedded in the crux of the ideology is the importance of moral responsibility and self-determination. The emphasis on moral responsibility can serve as a lever to stimulate positive individual social action such as academic progress. At the same time Adventist ideology employs a harsher tone when analysing the individual who has failed to make something of their life.

> If you should see an unfortunate specimen of humanity lying in the gutter, would you accuse his mother of giving birth to a derelict of society? Of course not. When that man was a baby, he was as pure and sweet as any other baby. As he grew to manhood, he chose to do evil. He made a derelict out of himself (Schwartz, 1970), p.120).

Schwartz discribes how the Seventh-Day Adventist ideology outlines a moral perspective towards secular affairs whilst at the same time encouraging its adherents to avoid certain kinds of secular affairs and attitudes. It instils comprehensive orientations towards practical matters, holding that a person who is saved not only lacks certain vices but also displays certain virtues. It is no surprise to the Adventist when they find themselves doing well academically, economically etc. Reiff (1967) discusses what he has termed the 'inner directive'. He points out that some religions instil a kind of awareness, a direction in its supporters. This inner directive will in fact guide the individual over all matters of conduct that may not have been discussed. The individual who has not acquired this inner drive will give in to despair, opening the heart's door to evil forces. One pastor argued that such a state would lead an individual to loose grasp of their destiny and ultimately they would be led to indulge in worldly pleasures which would inevitably lead to the loss of salvation.

Schwartz (1970) argues quite strongly that Adventists believe that they should live in this world purposefully and actively. Literature for youth encourages them to develop the traits which can be used to enhance their career prospects (*Encounter* and *Family Life* magazines). The Seventh-Day Adventist, according to Schwartz has a dominant fear of falling in the status system and a dominant hope of rising in it; these dominances are embedded in their theology and ideology. The fear of falling encourages the individual to avoid drink, sexual immorality etc and a hope of rising in the status system encourages academic achievement, social courtesies etc. In essence they associate righteousness with socially acceptable (middle class) life styles and wickedness with sensual (lower class) life styles.

In fact, when we trace the development of the SDA religion it is clear it came about during a time of religious anomie amongst a group of disappointed Christians. Furthermore, when we view its current position it is obvious to see that African-Caribbeans within the British context are an alienated minority group.

The above may leave the reader with the impression that the Adventist lives in fear of God's anger. To balance this perception one must also be mindful of the many Bible texts which reassure the Christian of God's caring, protective and loving nature (Psalm 23, Psalm 91 and Psalm 46).

Pentecostalist History

Pentecostalism, in its present form, as a self-consciously separate branch of Christianity, developed during the first decade of this century in the United States, England and Europe. Most of the Pentecostal churches trace their origin directly or indirectly to the 'Latter Rain' revival movement led by A J Tomlinson, founder of the Church of God. Other bodies indirectly derived from the Latter Rain revival include the Assemblies of God, United Pentecostal church, Pentecostal Holiness church, International Pentecostal Assemblies and Pentecostal Fire-Baptised Holiness church.

The success of the Pentecostal congregations in Britain, wholly organised and led by Caribbean immigrants, underlies the tragic failure of the traditional English churches to hold the allegiance of those immigrants who were already established Christians before coming to England. To see this failure in its true perspective one must bear in mind that in the Caribbean islands, Pentecostalists represent only 5% of the total Christian community. In his own research, Hill (1971) notes that a large number of those who were attracted to the Pentecostal sect during the first decade of immigration were formerly members of one or other of the six major branches of the Christian church.

Calley (1965) examined the rapid growth of immigrant Pentecostal congregations. He found that the New Testament Church of God, the largest of the Pentecostal immigrant sects in Britain, had a total of twenty-three congregations scattered throughout the country. Hill (1971) updated this research and found a total of sixty-one congregations with a total of 10,500, fifteen full-time ministers, a theological college training twenty students for the full-time ministry, a national headquarters in Birmingham. Forty-four groups were meeting in rented premises and seventeen owned their own church buildings.

Pentecostalist Theology

Pentecostalism stresses joy and optimism; for them salvation is open to all. Their worship is emotional and communal yet, interestingly, by contrast Jesus is sought individually during prayer. The Pentecostalists continually press to achieve spiritual purity. Although these groups prescribe fraternal solidarity, their theology promotes religious individualism.

Each person seeks his or her own consummation of a feeling of oneness with Jesus.

Unlike the Seventh-Day Adventist groups, these Pentecostal sects do not attempt to contain the individual believer in a complete theological structure specifying correct interpretations for all aspects of that individual's life. What is stressed is the personal meaning that is derived from the experience of conversion to Christ.

This sect does not attempt to build a theory which is committed to one interpretation of the meaning of human events. There does seem to be a body of contradictory views on all sorts of matters. Unlike Seventh-Day Adventists who use an established framework to orientate themselves to the world, the Pentecostals believe in the sudden intrusion of divine power in determining their social action.

Pentacostals believe that God's word is mysterious and that a pragmatic and intellectual approach to the study of the Bible is insufficient. Many informants desired a conversion experience as they felt that their lives were going down the drain. The Pentecostal ideology afforded them the opportunity to rise above their social deprivation. Willems (1969) noticed that converts to Pentecostalism in South America tended to come from the socially deprived groups. He comments that a crucial motive behind conversion is an unconscious identification with middle class respectability.

> Surely enough, the convert sheds his 'vices', but as he does he carefully rids himself of forms of behaviour which the society at large holds in disrepute. Drunken bouts, tavern brawls, wife-beating, illegitimacy, neglect of children and a disorganised home life, personal appearance suggesting neglect and uncleanliness, failure to improve poor housing conditions, and similar traits are often held against the lower classes. One may say, they are identified with lower class behaviour and therefore looked upon with a mixture of moral indignation and amused contempt. It seems that the Protestant convert is particularly sensitive to such criticism, for henceforward he carefully avoids 'disreputable forms of behaviour' (Schwartz, 1970, p.166).

Pentecostal Ideology

There appears to be a rejection of material and social trappings, yet in a subtle way the Pentecostals manifest their sense of social deprivation. They believe that they are financially secure and prosperous because they are God's servants and God owns the world. This philosophy leads them to build viewpoints that inspire to the realms of middle class respectability.

Pentecostalism which had not traditionally contained stable, concrete ideology to counterpoise racism and discrimination is beginning to adopt within its ranks some kind of policy. The disillusionment felt about the British education system has led many to set up 'Saturday schools' and adult literacy units. The idea that God helps those who help themselves has now spilled over into the wider issues of life. In London in particular, there are growing numbers of young professionals within the Pentecostal ranks and they are translating and articulating the ideas of this denomination within the framework of direction and positive action.

For the SDA and Pentecostals, religion could be viewed as the source of a resistance strategy which enables them to contend with the impact of racism within legal, legitimate boundaries. Unlike these sects, the Rastafarians' response to racism in Britain could be described as evasion or outright rejection. Adherents to the Rastafarian sect described other black people in Britain as 'misguided by European Christianity' or 'blinded by Babylon' (Cashmore, 1979). Rastafarian resistance can be evaluated via Fryer's (1984) use of the term — resistance is used synonymously with rebellion and refers to the uprisings of the early 1980s. In this book I use the term resistance as a conscious rejection of negative, racist stereotyping and a determination to struggle against the equally negative consequences of these stereotypes within socially accepted boundaries.

Rastafarian History

Rastas have for many years been labelled as 'religious fanatics', 'nuisances', an embarrassment to Jamaican people, or treacherous criminals who should be hung or jailed for treasonable acts against Jamaican society. By sporting 'dreadlocks', smoking ganja (marihuana), use of violent language of the Old Testament, the Rastafarians alarmed Jamaicans and attracted the attention of anthropologists.

The Rasta movement began to take shape in about 1980. They are seen as a politico-religious protest cult, who worship the Emperor Haille Selassie and aim to 'return' to Africa.

Rastafarian Theology

Basing their faith on the Old Testament prophecy, the Rastafarians assert that the black people of the world are the true tribe of Israel rather than those who falsely call themselves so: the Jews. They claim an African cultural heritage and identify with Negro people scattered all over the world. They insist that since their African ancestors were brought unwillingly to Jamaica as slaves, they should now be 'repatriated' to the land of their origin, Ethiopia, where reigns 'the first Asian King of Creation, the conquering Lion of the Tribe of Judah, God of the Black Race', or more generally to any part of Africa.

Rastafarian Ideology

The conscious effort by the Rastafarian to reject white British society and create a more meaningful existence needs to be seen within the context of two sociologys; of sect and subculture. Bernard (1983), researching the role of Rastafarian women, argued that the frame of reference used by this group gave them cultural and religious direction. Some writers have argued, however, that Rastafarianism seemed to build its philosophy on rejection and gives little space for the building of positive action. One ex-Rasta told me of his one 'Romantic' desire to return to 'Ethiopia' and the disillusionment he felt when he saw the condition of the people in that country. He was also shocked by his difficulty in accepting certain aspects of their lifestyle. He concluded painfully that he was still truly western. Rastafarianism for him had been a romantic perspective — it had drawn young black people together but failed to offer them any concrete alternative. He argued that the Rastafarianism alternative of 'opting out' of society did not enable them to positively 'attack' white society. Bernard (1983) examines the decline of the Rastafarian movement. She identifies reasons why the Islamic faith is regarded as a more attractive option. These points are discussed further in Chapter seven and the conclusion.

Concluding Comment

In this chapter I have presented some interrelated themes and issues concerning race and religion in Britain. The historical context was briefly described and the extent to which the philosophies and environment of black sects might empower, or enable members to strive for academic success, has also been outlined. To test out this idea effectively, I need to employ a research method or approach which gives individuals the opportunity to reflect on their experience as members of these sects. Chapter three presents an argument for the appropriateness of a particular form of a qualitative approach to this research, namely the life history method.

Chapter 3

Methodology

This chapter is divided into subsections to enable the reader to identify the separate but equally significant methodological issues of concern in this study. A brief overview of the current status and the use of the life history approach is followed by an examination of a range of research 'problems'. Milroy's (1987) social network analysis provides the study with a rationale for locating the subjects while Denzin's (1989) research notions provide a framework for analysis so both writers' works are outlined and discussed. An account of the process of data collection is an important part of any methodological chapter, so there is also a brief outline of this process.

The researcher's position is often excluded from the methodology of studies. However, the use which feminist sociologists have made of the 'Personal is Political' concept in relation to research methodology rightly examines the motives of the researcher. Their conviction that the omittance of the 'personal' from the process of even the most exploratory of qualitative projects has seriously hindered and distorted 'discovery', thus rendering the 'surprises' of such work 'not at all surprising', has had a significant impact on my work. The 'personal' in this study is very much a part of the theoretical and I feel it is important that this is understood. An appreciation of the centrality of the reflexivity of this approach has led me to include my own life history. Through this presentation of the 'personal self', my theoretical and methodological biases may be recognised (Woods, 1986, p.43).

Historical Position of the Life History Approach

Since the time of the Chicago school (for overview see Bogardus, 1933; Blumer, 1939; Hammersley, 1989), social scientists have used life documents in many ways to investigate various aspects of social existence. During the 1950s and 1960s such writers as Goffman and Garfinkel looked at face to face interaction and its interpretation. They explored taken for granted meanings and underlying assumptions in the interaction process. Becker (1963) and Kitsuse (1963) are two other social scientists who have come to be known as 'labelling theorists' because of the extent to which they examined the social label given to those regarded by society as 'deviant'. Over time the value given to the 'subject's' view has gained in importance.

Despite Thomas and Znanaiecki's (1958) assertion that the life history technique could be regarded as producing the 'perfect' type of sociological material, this method has functioned at the margins of sociological acceptability for some time. Currently the life history approach is experiencing a resurgence and is being used to investigate areas of social policy (Gibson and Burrows, 1986), social work practice (Marsh et el, 1986), race relations (Bryan et al, 1985). In the field of educational research, the notion of giving regard to the subject's perception is becoming viable and valid. It could be said that educational researchers are acting as pioneers of the movement. A number of these studies address the needs of black children in primary and secondary schools, such as Mac an Ghaill (1988), Gillborn (1990). Others evaluate factors which influence teachers' career directions: Sikes et al (1987), Aspinwall (1985), Hinchliffe (1985), Evetts (1990). Research methods of this nature have recently been used a great deal to examine the experiences of individuals and groups whose perceptions have previously been accorded little value and a number of these research projects are referred to.

The life history/biographical approach, then, is employed by many disciplines. However it is noteworthy that this approach is not homogeneous but represents a variety of views, and a range of perspectives; as the interpretative approach has developed it has subdivided and found varied areas of focus. In his critical analysis of this method, Denzin (1989) states:

> Some impose a grand theoretical structure upon the interpretative enterprise, seeking a totalising theory of human societies, human action and human history. Still others formulate ideal types and assess their theory-interpretative work in terms of such concepts as empirical adequacy, empirical validity, and so on. Some eschew such subjective concepts as self, intention, meaning and motive, and search only for invariant, publicly observable patterns of action (p.14).

Place of the life history method in social theory and methodology

As a number of social scientists have developed an interest in a phenomenological approach, their attitude toward traditional, positivist approaches have ranged from tolerance to outright condemnation. Hammersley (1989) in his critical historical analysis of the development of social science notes that however justified qualitative researchers may be in their criticism of positivism, there is the possibility that qualitative researchers may in their complacency produce the same problems contained in their accusations. Hammersley raises fundamental questions about the nature and role of qualitative research methods when he asks:

> Is ethnography devoted to description or is it also concerned with developing valid explanations and theories. If the latter, what are the means by which the validity of explanations and theories are assessed? If operationalisation of concrete indicators are to be avoided, how can concepts be clarified and related to data? And, perhaps most fundamental of all, how do ethnographers know that quantitative research fails to capture social reality, what access do they have to the latter? If that access is through everyday experience of the social world, what justification is there for taking this to represent the true nature of that world? (pp.3-4).

I have referred to the beginnings of the life history method and noted the positivist approach taken by the Chicago school. The method has not developed in a homogeneous fashion since, but generally speaking, it now rests on the phenomenological/interpretative tradition. This work's use of the life history method seeks to examine such subjective concepts as self, meaning and motive. However, as positivism and phenomenology are not necessarily alternative perspectives when developing theory or choosing a method, a research project can make use of both, adopting and adapting methods associated with each school of thought.

The focus of this study is the need to give a voice to the subject. Given the current 'race-relations' debate (Gilroy, 1981, Hall, 1980), critics might identify in this work an emphasis which appears to advocate a 'blaming the victim' approach. Clearly a tension exists between the need to evaluate the structural factors which impact on the lives of the subjects represented here, and the need to acknowledge the significant place of the individual's interpretation of their own reality. Avoiding the tendency, on the one hand, to pathologise the individual, and on the other, to focus only on the socially constructed oppressive system that impacts on the lives of black people, is a theme which underpins this work. This book recognises but does not seek to resolve this tension.

In this subsection I wish to examine a range of arguments concerning this and other analogous methods, highlighting how concerns about these methods may impinge upon the study. A discussion of ethical, political, personal, technical and social science problems will attempt to identify a wider list of general methodological issues which all research must confront.

Social science problems

Questions about social science issues explore the 'why' questions of social research. They deal with choices made and the justification for those choices in the research arena. Why should this research choose to use a certain method in preference to other methods? As already stated, the distinction between positivist and phenomenological research methodologies are not as clear-cut as is often implied; rather they are often placed at the opposite ends of the spectrum for the purposes of emphasis and illustration. Methods of data collection and means of interpretation cannot be neatly categorised as belonging to one perspective or another. However certain methods are often regarded as more appropriate by advocates of different perspectives. A number of researchers note that, whereas statistical methods may be able to deal with situations where behaviour has become routinised so that it is eventually standardised and repetitive, these methods are not adequate to deal with creativity and innovation. Burgess (1982) suggested that,

> quantitative methods deal in the main with the cruder, more external aspects of human behaviour, but a more sympathetic and discerning method is necessary to probe beneath the surface and to depict and analyse the inner life of the person (p.112).

Burgess (1982) asked,

> How can attitudes, the basic subject matter of human nature and society, be stated numerically? How can the so-called intangible facts of life, its qualitative aspects, be apprehended by so crude an instrument as statistics? What figure will measure the degree of affection between husband and wife, or the nature and intensity of a father's pride in his children, or qualities of personalities like charm, loyalty and leadership? (pp.111-112).

As Farraday and Plummer (1979) suggest, the life history technique focuses upon areas which are often neglected in other forms of sociological work. Most notably the life history technique is able to grapple with the problems of the subjective reality of the individual.

> In the life history is revealed, as in no other way, the inner life of the person, his moral struggles, his successes and failure in securing his destiny in a world too often at variance with his hopes and ideals. (Burgess, 1968 p.776; quoted in Farraday and Plummer, 1979).

In their quest for generalisation, most methods of social science tend to impose order and rationality upon experiences and worlds that are ambiguous, chaotic and problematic in reality. It is clear that the life history technique does not approach theory in any 'grand or formal' way; it makes no claim to representativeness and is usually viewed as an ideographic method. However the life history technique is particular suited to discovering the confusions, ambiguities, and contradictions that are displayed in everyday experience. It can therefore serve as a useful correction to the mainstream of social science which focuses on uniformity and regularity. The life history method strives towards locating the individual first of all in his/her overall life experience in the immediate social context, prior to linking it with a broader socio-historical framework.

For some researchers the life history method provides an alternative approach to more conventional methods used by the social science community: a tool which identifies issues which may be later studied more formally. For example Farraday and Plummer (1979) observes that:

> In the areas of enquiry about which little is known, the life history technique can become a sensitising tool to the kinds of issues and problems involved in the field. It is specially useful in the areas in which the conceptualisation of problems has been little worked out.

For other sociologists the focus of the method is to examine and unpick those life experiences that individuals deem to have altered, shaped and given meaning to their lives. Denzin (1989) and others regard each social interaction as unique and they aim to study these reactions from the point of view of the participant.

However, while extolling the virtues of the method, its exploratory role, its ability to grapple with subjective reality, researchers calculate the cost of these benefits as they acknowledge the extent to which these attributes are said to give the method an unacknowledged theoretical bias. There is no intrinsic disconnection of the life history from the theoretical work. In defence, qualitative researchers stress the diversity and variability of social life and its concern with capturing the myriad perspectives of those in the social world. They suggest that if we are to understand the social world, rather than aping the natural sciences, we must attune our methods of inquiry to its nature. Given that the object of science is to aid in the understanding of human activity, if a piece of research helps in that process of unlocking some aspects of this complex universe of 'man and nature', it has served its purpose.

This book seeks to examine a number of intangible social phenomena from the view of the subject. It is based on the assumptions that the meanings that experiences have for people are not universal or fixed. The study holds to the view that meanings are:

> developed in the process of social interaction in the particular cultural settings and are therefore variable between and within societies. Individuals, also groups, occupying or living in the same spatial location may be people living side by side yet be living in different worlds (Blumer, 1969, p.11).

Why might it be that some black people experience the British education system as an insurmountable hurdle which continuously blocks their progress, while others achieve their educational goals while living in the same racist climate? This question is a central area of discussion.

Practical and technical problems

When considering the practical and technical problems of the life history method, we are concerned with how the research gets executed. Many of the technical problems, for example, choice of data gathering method, interviewing, dealing with transcripts, problems of validity and representativeness, are the same as those faced by other ethnographic methods. Other practical problems, for example, finding and choosing subjects and understanding their motives for participation, are specially relevant to the life history method. In an attempt to evaluate the motivation of individuals who participate in first-person life documents, Allport (1942) lists thirteen reasons why participants may agree to take part in a study. The list not only indicates the ways in which individuals may be encouraged to participate but also provides a checklist for possible vices, such as exhibitionism and catharsis.

Those researchers who are particularly influenced by a structural functionalist framework regard the issue of 'contamination' of the data as fundamental to the process of the research. Denzin (1989) notes that because many such researchers have given their attention to the problems of validity, reliability and theory development, the results of their work is often a trivialisation and distortion of the original interest of the method.

Farraday and Plummer (1979) suggest that a continuum may be used to locate the extent to which the sociologist imposes his or her own analytical devices upon the subject or the extent to which the subject's own world is allowed to stand 'uncontaminated'. At one extreme of the continuum, the sociologist will be engaging in 'Armchair Theory', constructing his or her own account independently of the subject. At the other extreme, there is reliance on the subject's own account with no researcher analysis attached, eg autobiographies diaries etc. Farraday and Plummer suggest that the researcher who uses life histories can legitimately move through any stages of this continuum as long as they publicly acknowledge how far they are 'contaminating' the data. Sociologists should therefore attempt to make explicit the nature of interpretation that has taken place. When considering the issue of 'contamination' one should identify the value of the inter flow between subject and sociologist. Acknowledging that '*only the representations of experience can ever be captured*', Denzin (1989) and other researchers are less concerned with positivist notions of contamination. Rather they applaud the valuable role of the sociologist in assisting the subject to 'tell her/his story', emphasising the need for 'thick' rather than 'thin' descriptions and interpretations.

Ethical and political issues

Research reports are often written in a technical style with no hint of the ethical, political or personal problems which confronted the researcher during the research (Farraday and Plummer, 1979). Issues of friendships, relationships, confidentiality, conflicts of interest need constant assessment and reassessment. Proponents of the positivist tradition have argued that levels of generalisation are as near value-free as possible. However even this form of research is often based on social constructs, such as 'childhood'. Research designs are chosen because children are 'known' to be immature. Concepts, common sense knowledge, and stereotypes about children influence what is said to be value-free research. In the interpretative tradition, sense is made out of an event by giving meaning to an observable phenomenon. As a participant observer for example, gradations of immersion allows the researcher to assess to what extent as an outsider they may have to learn to 'be a friend', or remain an outsider, in the research situation. At this point we could consider the extent to which a white researcher can engage in a research project about black people.

It could be that a white person who is working through a deconstructing and consciousness-raising excercise in learning about racism might question their own suitability in engaging in anti-racist behaviour. Such a person may conclude that the personal and institutional power imbalance present in a research relationship can be dealt with as an academic exercise. They may regard it as possible to separate out the 'everyday self' from the 'research self' (Frankenberg, 1963). A 'non-racist' researcher may feel that they can do as good a job as a black researcher; they may well consider 'class' more significant than 'race'. Many white researchers in this area suggest that, as an 'outsider', they can be more objective and perceptive than those who are embroiled in the experience. Indeed a number of white researchers who are not burdened with collective white guilt argue that to marginalise issues of race, leaving it only to black people, is unprofessional and academically unsound.

The reflexivity of the ethnographic approach led Mac an Ghaill (1988) to reconsider his area of focus in his research project and acknowledged the significance of the role of the researcher. He suggests that in part he was able to break down the racial and age barriers by visiting the homes of his subjects, accompanying them to places such as the cinema, theatre, and anti-racist meetings. He even attended evening classes in an attempt to learn to speak an Asian language and tried out his newly acquired skill on his subjects. Being Irish was also deemed to be an advantage, as the black pupils related to and understood his views and experiences of British imperialist interventions. Despite all he brought to the research relationship, Mac an Ghaill (1989) acknowledged that:

> In the past researchers have failed to take into account how their relationship with black respondents may be influenced by racism... It should be added that my interaction with black females may also be informed by sexism (p.181).

By adopting a theoretical position that sees racism and sexism as the major barriers to the schooling of black youths, Mac an Ghaill regards his approach as sensitive to the question of how social location in a stratified society, including differential power relations, can influence one's perceptions and therefore influences his own study.

Given that research findings are in part a product of the interaction between researcher and subject, the relationship between these individuals is significant. It could be that as 'race', age, and gender are integral facets of any human relationship, some research settings are closed to some researchers. The ethical and even moral consideration of negotiating with the subject is part and parcel of the research package. However Burgess (1982) notes that often the researcher simply 'gets the data and leaves the subject bleeding on the sidewalk'. Questions about trust, informed consent, and researcher responsibility permeate this discussion.

Farraday and Plummer (1979) found that as their research progressed they found no neat mechanism for coping with the strains which such problems presented. During the earlier stages of this study I felt somewhat reassured to learn from seasoned researchers like Farraday and Plummer that the elements of ambiguity and uncertainty inherent in this type of research may diminish over time, as practical manageable areas in which to concentrate emerge. A detailed description of the data collection process and the specific problems faced in this thesis follow later in this chapter. First I explore an approach formulated by Milroy (1987) which influenced the methodology used in this research.

Social networking — a rationale for subject identification and data collection

When faced with a similar range of difficulties, Milroy (1987) formulated the social network system, a method which took account of common concerns encountered when research projects have a qualitative bias. As a sociolinguist, Milroy sought to examine the manner in which patterns of linguistic variation characterise particular groups within a complex, urban community during an explosive socio-political era. She demonstrates how an ethnographic approach to the socio-linguistic fieldwork takes into consideration issues which would not be given the weight they deserved if a purely quantitative approached were implemented. As she points out:

> Despite the development of special techniques a linguistic investigator invariably encounters the problem which Labov has aptly named 'the observer's paradox'. Language in the community can be studied only by collecting large volumes of natural speech on good quality recording; yet, a stranger who attempts to obtain these, dramatically changes the character of the phenomenon he is observing. When a further axiom is accepted, that the database should be the wider community and not a circle of friends or a captive population (such as school children or hospital patients) the investigator must immediately consider the problem of obtaining representative data... As Sankoft has pointed out, 'data collected in this manner may be limited grammatically as well as stylistically... ' (p.40).

By engineering the theory of social networks, Milroy overcame considerable research difficulties. As a methodological principle underlying fieldwork strategies, the notion of social network operates on the premise that:

> people interact meaningfully as individuals in addition to forming parts of structured, functional institutions such as classes, castes or occupational groups (pp.45-46).

Importance is given to structural features of human relationships. Social or personal attributes of the individuals receive little weight and the central focus lies around the characteristics of the linkages which bind individuals to each other. She outlines the process as follows:

> Each person may be viewed as a focus from which lines radiate to points (person with whom he is in contact). These persons who are linked directly to ego may be characterised as belonging to his first order network zone. Each of these people may be in contact with others whom ego does not know, but could come into contact with via his first order zone. These more distantly connected persons form ego's second order zone (pp.46-47).

Milroy gives some consideration to the issue of exchange, rights and obligations, noting that a social network acts as a mechanism both for exchanging goods and services and for conferring rights, imposing corresponding obligations upon its members. Using this framework most speech events could be deemed as 'tokens of exchange' (Milroy, 1987).

To engage a subject in a prolonged relationship for the sake of the study, a fieldworker would need to proffer such tokens as will establish and maintain exchanges in relationships. Labov (1972) found that people will generally be willing to talk voluntarily if the interviewer is sympathetic and genuinely interested. For Labov, tokens of exchange included sympathy and a boost to the informant's self-esteem. Wolfson's research (1976) could be presented as an example of an unsuccessful attempt to establish or exchange relationships. Wolfson evaluated the process and results of the interview and concluded that asymmetrical age-sex relationships between participants were responsible for the lack of success. Labov (1972) also noted the significance of asymmetrical race relationships between participants. This observation led him to use an 'insider' and an 'outsider' fieldworker. Milroy (1987) challenges Wolfson's (1976) conclusions, suggesting that it is quite possible to record large volumes of speech even where these asymmetrical relationships exist.

Within the parameters of the exchange theory, Milroy (1980) postulates that to engage in any meaningful prolonged interaction, the fieldworker is 'obliged' to offer goods and/or services equal in value to that he/she wishes the informant to give. In Wolfson's case the restaurant owner was under no obligation to provide her with goods and services, seeing that Wolfson was unable to offer anything in exchange! In this way the concept of obligation further clarifies the notion of exchange within such relationships. It is appropriate to explore to what extent the present study could benefit from Milroy's (1980) theoretical position.

The use of social networks in this study

Using social networks in the present study might at first be viewed as a functional decision, one which would minimise the problem or the logistics of locating an appropriate group or set of individuals. However, noting that the role of the fieldworker was central to good data collection, I acknowledged that my role and position in the community was an invaluable resource. I regarded the fact that subjects and researcher share a common culture as a potential strength rather than difficulty. I could offer certain goods and services which might satisfy Milroy's notion of obligation and exchange between the life history subject and myself. As we were all individuals who were to some extent engaged in academic pursuits we would have interests in common. The sharing of materials, resources (audio visual materials, literature) proved to be central to our relationship, as did shared discussion about: career movements, shared past and recent memories of the Caribbean, cultural and racial experiences, past and present religious experiences, 'gossip' or informal news about events within our communities.

The reciprocal and mutual support of fieldworker and subject was evidenced through offers of sympathy, empathy and boosts to self-esteem and these tokens of exchange assisted in establishing and maintaining the interactions. Along with Labov (1972), I register the importance of the 'race' dimension in the relationship between subject and researcher. We saw how Mac an Ghaill (1988) examined a range of methodological and political issues raised when the study of black females is undertaken by a white male researcher, although Milroy (1980) discount's Wolfson's (1976) failures as purely a result of asymmetrical relationships between participants. However, she (Milroy p.84) does not deny the significant place of symmetrical relationships in ensuring satisfactory data collection.

Denzin's research notions — a framework for analysis

More specific consideration is needed of 'how to' examine life history data. This section begins this examination by outlining and then selecting relevant aspects from Denzin's (1989) research notions of Thick and Thin descriptions and Thick and Thin interpretations as they are used in his presentation of interpretative interactionism. Where Milroy (1987) provided a framework for data collection, Denzin offers a grounded approach to handling a mass of raw data. Limitations to his approach are examined and the data collection process for this work described and further explored.

Denzin's (1989) use of the research devices of Thick and Thin description and Thick and Thin interpretation are specifically geared towards exploring and understanding a particular range of social phenomena. A close examination of an individual's own perception of their experiences is the core feature of Denzin's interpretative interactionism. He uses Thick and Thin descriptions and Thick and Thin interpretations to assist in this evaluation. Denzin's research devices provide me with a viable and apparently sensitive approach to the analysis of the data. For, central both to Denzin's and my work is the importance of interpretation, subjectivity and understanding, as key features of social life. Our subject areas reflect similar themes, which concern the aspects of human relationships which require some exploration if future negative experiences are to be avoided and positive experiences fostered.

Denzin comments that:

> there is nothing magical or mysterious about this method. It involves using skills any person already has — namely, the ability to talk and listen to others including yourself (p.12).

In making a distinction between Thick and Thin descriptions, Denzin provides the researcher and reader with an understanding of the centrality and significance of the subject's perception of their experience. In Thick description, the voices, feelings, actions and meanings of interacting individuals are heard. Thick description goes beyond Thin description in that it offers more than mere facts; Thin descriptions do not present lived experiences.

In recent decades a number of sociologists have emphasised their movement away from established thinking by reclassifying their work and coining new terms. Creative sociology, existential sociology and Denzin's own interpretative interactionism are examples of this. In his understanding of human interaction, Denzin (1989) utilises many of the core themes present in the symbolic interactionist approach. To these central themes he adds the notion of problematic interaction. This kind of interaction, he proposes, alters how persons define themselves and their relations with others. Interpretative interactionism, then, provides the channel through which meaning can be confirmed and an understanding of problematic symbolic interactions be gained.

According to Plummer (1983), any genuine commitment to examine issues of oppression such as wife-beating (one of Denzin's research areas) should be applauded. Like other researchers before him, Denzin uses the medium of qualitative research to give voice to 'the marginal underdog'. However Denzin's claim to take seriously a feminist stance, thus providing a sensitive gender bias could be challenged, as he appears to neglect the need to marry the subject's voice sufficiently to structural concerns. Simply listening to the woman's account and re-examining the institutions set up to deal with the aftermath of her experience is unlikely to satisfy feminist sociologists of a genuine feminist stance. Denzin gives value to the ways in which women experience their existence, but fails to expose the social relations and social forces responsible for creating this state of affairs. Feminists see no divide between material and political consideration and women's emotional welfare (Butler and Wintram, 1991).

At the heart of feminism is the simple idea that there are not two sorts of people in the world, the superior and the inferior or, in terms of power relations, the dominant and the subdominant. We are equal irrespective of our gender. Social relations that obliterate this fact must therefore be transformed and recreated in ways that reflect equality in terms of gender. In keeping with this, a feminist stance endorses egalitarianism in all social dimensions. Class cannot be ignored. Black women have upbraided the white sister for falling into the trap of racism by omission, in assuming that sisterhood encompassed the interests of black women and white alike. Feminists view deeply entrenched patriarchal social relations rather than men as the prime target for change. Key to the feminist movement has been the way in which work on defining and re-defining social problems has led to the development of a whole range of initiatives, eg rape crisis centres and well women clinics. Denzin neglects this wider debate.

The extent to which Denzin deems it necessary to locate subjects within their social setting appears to be restricted to a consideration of their martial status or chronological age. He states that:

> Once found, subjects must be located within the social structure of the setting — that is married, divorced, old, young, men, women and so on. This means that the researcher must identify the categories and meanings that are used to define persons in that situation (p.44).

Throughout the various steps of interpretation, Denzin neglects opportunities to anchor the subject's view securely in wider sociological and social concerns and fails to examine the social control function of the caring services. Their current policy and practice demonstrate that these agencies continue to play a diversionary role in respect to social deprivation. Denzin's acknowledgement that 'an understanding and interpretation of everyday life must consider the gendered, situated, structural and practical features of that world' may be counter-productive, in that he risks being accused of perpetuating a line of thinking which may result in the 'blaming of the victim'. Plummer (1990) notes that: 'It could lead some unsympathetic readers to believe that interactionism still remains too unwedded to the wider social concerns of sociology' (p.797).

Denzin's approach provides a useful 'take off point' (Plummer, 1990) for those wishing to give value to the subjective. However this work attempts to include a wider consideration of the social group represented by these individuals. It is important to identify and give some consideration to a range of structural issues which impact on their lives, as well as listening to the personal account of what shaped or conditioned their choices. It may be that the problem here is one of emphasis; the subjective is worthy of the academic. This is not in dispute. At the same time, it is equally important to locate the individual in a wider social system and acknowledge issues of social construction.

By using certain research techniques, Denzin highlights certain areas of concern. He regards Thin descriptions as glossing, or giving superficial, partial and sparse accounts of events. They use a few words to describe complex, meaningful events. In this sense they let 'big words', often social science terms, second order and experience-distant concepts (Denzin p.87), do the work of many 'little words'. The result is often to hide experience rather than illuminating it. Given the focus of this study, and my aim to provide the fullest possible account of the subject's view, Thin descriptions will not be used, as they do not assist in this process.

The use of Thick description in this thesis

While acknowledging the limitations of this approach, this work has from the outset identified its commitment to presenting the subject's account. Liberal use of glosses and summaries which relegate the subject's point of view would not foster the project's central thrust.

I use a macro-historical approach, in the sense that each life history subject relives their biographies. They focus on their educational experiences and the ways in which their relationship with family members, school staff and other significant adults impact on their lives. Whereas Denzin (1989) works at a 'fine grained' exploration of events, I look at experiences over time, using a much 'broader brush' on a 'wider canvas'. My aim is to acknowledge the interactional, situational and intrusive nature of the approach. In their presentation of their accounts, the subjects do use glossed Thick description, they make liberal use of summaries, and often give superficial, partial and sparse accounts of events.

Researchers commonly 'promise more than they actually deliver'. Having been sensitised to the parameters and nuances of the ethnographic view, I regard Denzin's concepts as a guide to my methodology, since I do not claim to have achieved the very difficult result of Thick description. Indeed I am not sure whether Denzin himself achieves his aims. The role of and need for interpretation will be further discussed in a later chapter but first there is a need to establish how the data was collected the source of the Thick description. An appreciation of the reflexive nature of qualitative research leads me to conclude this chapter with my autobiography thus firmly locating the possible biases that may arise from the researcher's own position (Mac an Ghaill, 1989, Denzin, 1989).

Process of data collection for this work

Over a period of time I observed an obvious discrepancy between the education experience of many black people with whom I associated and public information which appeared to be taken for granted. While many black people I knew, including members of my own family, were excelling in the academic field, research projects, media reports and other ongoing debates seemed to focus on the 'problems' faced by black children in

British schools. The unprecedented levels of 'underachievement' experienced by black pupils in their school careers was central to this debate.

This initial observation of apparent discrepancy required further exploration to establish the extent to which there was any substance to this perceived phenomenon. At the outset I sent questionnaires to a number of individuals whom I identified as academic achievers. These individuals, with at least a first degree, were invited to complete and return the questionnaire. The mailing list included personal acquaintances, contacts through friends, polytechnic and university members of African-Caribbean Associations. After receiving a number of these responses, it became apparent that this research method did not give the respondents the scope to present a complete picture of a somewhat complicated issue. Many individuals felt that it was necessary to include additional sheets which expanded a number of areas. In trying to solve this research problem I discovered the value of the much neglected qualitative approach. It became clear 'as in a vision' that the notions I held about the austere and clinical nature of all research methods were inaccurate. In fact, although neglected, research methods which permitted the subject to relate their account of school days, family life, employment — including or excluding any aspects of the account they deemed crucial to understanding the full story — were available and indeed enjoying a resurgence.

I asked a number of those who had responded to the questionnaire if they would be interested in participating in further exploration of the issues on a personal level. None of the respondents declined the offer, despite the time-consuming nature of the project and my wish to audio tape the sessions. They seemed keen to put aside time to have further discussions. When arranging the interviews, I explained to the respondents the purpose of the sessions, stressing the extent to which personal details would remain confidential. Indeed, anonymity would be assured, even if the project might suffer due to the need to omit obvious identifying factors.

It is probably true to say that the earlier interviews did not flow as smoothly as the later ones, when I felt more at ease with the research method, so allowed the respondents to roam more freely to and fro across their career map without feeling the compulsion to probe, direct and unnecessarily structure the sessions. On occasions I intervened, seeking confirmation, elaboration and asking more questions. In the earlier sessions I agonised about my proximity to the project. Would any preconceptions I had influence my approach? Would the questions I asked be sufficiently open-ended? Was the subject so 'dear to my heart' that I would unwittingly influence the respondents? Listening to the taped conversations, I am sometimes astonished at my convoluted questions, caused by my anxieties about over-influencing the subject's view. These concerns about the quality of the data collected in the earlier sessions have led me to value the discussions as aids to raising and clarifying issues. However, verbatim quotes from these sessions will not be used in the Thick descriptions.

As the sessions progressed it became clear that I would need to be more confident about the nature of our interactions. A clear understanding of the nature of these sessions helped me to develop a sense of confidence. A brief look at the variation in terminology was helpful. Woods (1985, p.16) calls his interactions 'conversations', noting that they are definitely not interviews but more akin to participant observations, as empathy and sharing life accounts were significant elements. 'Interviews' appear to be a limited description of what occurred, although unstructured interviewing is a term often used to describe relatively open-ended discussions. Zweig (1948) seems to operate at the furthest point of the continuum when he refers to 'casual talks' (p.1). Although we shared opinions, and I shared, to a limited degree, accounts of my life history, to a limited degree, and expressed empathy, the focus of our discussions was always the respondent's biography. Stenhouse's (1980) use of the term 'one-sided conversation' best describes the nature of the interactions. I informed the subjects that they could omit or include any key influences in terms of people or events which might shed light on their academic achievement.

On average I met each respondent twice for sessions of an hour to two hours. It was important to place some realistic limit on the number of times we would meet and to ensure that the time commitment was clear from the start. This is not common practice amongst biographers. For example, Woods continued to meet the teachers in his study until a 'natural conclusion' was reached. Personal and professional duties sometimes caused the rescheduling of sessions but they were usually held within three weeks. When delays occurred, it felt helpful for me to remind the subject of our previous conversation. Rarely had they forgotten it, on the contrary they had used the ensuing period to reflect on it. This period of reflection often enhanced the second session. Before and at the close of a session the subjects and I often talked about the process of data collection and the value we perceived the project might hold. In general, the focus on educational achievement rather than the 'underachievement' of the black community was applauded as beneficial and valid. Concerns about the possible misreading of the project's intent and the information it presented were examined. At an initial introductory meeting we discussed issues such as: could or would readers accuse the author of operating a 'blame the victim' approach? Subjects did not allow this eventuality to discourage them. On the contrary, the opportunity for them to work with a black researcher who knows 'the field' and could not be described as 'an airport sociologist' (Ahmed, 1986), to unpick this area of black experience was regarded as invaluable.

Similarly, a number of the respondents confided that they found this space and the opportunity to off-load and reflect on their own life experiences cathartic. On a number of occasions they recalled painful experiences and used the sessions as an opportunity to relive, make sense of, and work through incidents which had remained areas of unresolved personal tension. Respondents also shared incidents and experiences not previously shared but which had caused shame, reservation and even retardation in the widest sense. Nevertheless these conversations did not drift into counselling sessions. However, the respondents and I acknowledged the need for formal and informal support networks for black academics and professionals.

Transcribing

Each session was audio-taped. I did not make notes during the conversations lest it appear intrusive and distracting. I did begin my first session with each respondent by obtaining from them a career map, a summary of main dates, geographical locations and information about family members. After each conversation I made notes of what appeared to me to be major issues of discussion. These notes played a significant role in the task of compiling and identifying the thematic areas. Although I was advised that there was no need to transcribe all the tapes, I found that by listening to the taped interviews I became helpfully familiar with the data. Transcribing each session verbatim was a painfully slow exercise but this also permitted the data to seep into my memory. By writing out the views and perceptions of the life history subjects, I hoped to obtain written copies of their accounts, which could be presented without being glossed or summarised and which were minimally influenced by the researcher.

Each of the methods of recording contributed differently to my understanding of the process. The concentration at the time and recollection afterwards assisted in the process of absorption. In common with many researchers, I found that a tape-recording and even more a transcript only partly conveys what occurs in these sessions. There is considerable loss at each stage of the process. A tape-recording gives the tone of voice, the speed of speech and emphasis but cannot fully convey the emotions involved or any of the non-verbal communication. Change of tone can reflect change of mood or only the speaker moving closer to or further from the microphones.

The 'loss' in transcribing a written account is even greater. Spoken conversation does not easily translate into writing. In transcribing what was said there is a problem of with punctuation. Speech does not use the same neat sentence patterns as written language. There is a real problem in deciding whether a pause needs a stop or a comma or whether to leave punctuation out altogether. Rethinkings in mid-stream can make the sense of what was said obscure when it is written down, although it may not have seemed so as the words were being spoken. I decided that every spoken word, even if it looked confusing in print, should be written down. I did not note 'ums' or 'ers' as I felt that they would impede the reading of the text. Instead, I sometimes noted these interjections thus... to indicate hesitation. I did not always add bracketed descriptions such as 'with sadness' or 'joking'.

Plummer (1979) declares that his offer of guidelines for doing life histories cannot be regarded as rigid, for this kind of work involves ambiguities and unpredictability. He identifies the gathering of personal documents in social science as a long and complicated process and admits to only raising a few issues in an attempt to sensitise the intending researcher to some possible areas of concern. For convenience alone, he depicts five broad processes. Plummer's (1979) five point plan at first glance seems to be presented as a neatly ordered list, and it appears appealing as an aid in organising the present study. However, this 'order' is tempered by the statement that the process listed is not necessarily sequential. Indeed the very reflexivity of the method would ensure that the steps would run side by side. Understanding the need to be rigorous with the technical aspects of 'writing up' the data is essential if the work is to be acceptable to a range of readers. Equally important is the personal position of the researcher. The following section is a brief outline of my own life history. In the writing and reading of the section many 'hidden influences' which impact on the study might be thus unravelled. The first section of the concluding discussion further examines aspects of my own educational experiences.

Autobiography

Grumet (1981) examines the personal benefits gained from the reflexive process of collecting biographies, by asking the questions: How does my present situation influence my understanding of the past? How do my hopes and dreads determine what it is in my past that I remember? How does it provide the future? What is it we find when we reclaim our experience? (Grumet, 1981, p.115).

Woods (1986) writing on how to begin an ethnographic study, advises:

> Since so much of the ethnographer is involved within the research, it is as well to subject the person, including one's motives, to scrutiny. (1986), p.20)

With this advice in mind I offer my reflection on my own life history.

The first six years of my life were spent in the beautiful island of Jamaica. When we (my sister and I) were three and a half or four we were sent to private nursery (Mrs B's front room). I have early memories of being well turned out in the clean and ironed blue and white uniforms, while the boys wore khaki-green outfits. Everyone looked spotless and behaved angelically. In Jamaica education was 'serious business'. Although the school fees for this age group were not extortionate it was a sacrifice for most parents to find extra finance. Looking after your pencil and slate or books was your own responsibility as they were relatively expensive to replace.

Coming to England was exciting. , We (My sister and I) were going to see our mum, who had left the island a few years before. We travelled alone as unaccompanied minors on the aircraft but were thoroughly 'spoilt' by the cabin staff. However, England itself was a real disappointment. Snow looked like a fun thing to play with, but it was cold, and was one factor that kept us 'indoors'; a new experience.

Our primary and junior education was uneventful. That is we coped with or tried to ignore the unkind jokes, sarcasm, and what felt like frequent unnecessary corrections to our pronunciation. 'Film not flim, certificate not cerfiticate' etc. Mum kept in touch with the teachers and did extra maths and English with us at home. She consistently reinforced the message about the importance and value of education. When we wanted to spend too long in front of the television she would say '*Dem have dem job already you jus a wok fe yours... go read you book*'. We didn't rebel — in fact we both enjoyed learning and 'got on' with the teachers: Mr Elliot, Mr Worthington, Miss Maguire, Mr Lush the headmaster with squeaky shoes. They all had their idiosyncratic ways which entertained, frustrated, offended and educated us.

Our secondary school was known to be a 'good comp' and was situated in an area where African-Caribbeans and Asians were well represented. I had been offered a place at the local grammar school but Mum had allowed me the choice of accepting the offer or joining my sister at the local comprehensive school. Subsequently mum and I have spoken about how uninformed she had been about the 'advantages' of a grammar school. I would have been one of a few black girls in that 'posh' school. Anyway I went into the 'grammar stream' of the comprehensive school. The cohort were streamed into six groups plus remedial (1.1-1.6). I had never thought of my self as clever (I still don't) and even the offer of going to the posh school hadn't made a significant impression on me. However being placed in 1.1 was an awakening — I was sure I didn't belong there. There were two other black girls in my class, Beverly and Angela. While I was overwhelmed at my own position, I couldn't work out why there were not more black girls in the top streams. Why were most of them in 1.4-1.6 and the remedial classes? These were overshadowing questions which haunted me long before I 'entered the field' (Malinowski, 1922).

The whole class were constantly reminded to 'behave well', 'set a good example', 'represent the school in a positive light' etc. On reflection I think that these reminders were unnecessary because we 'felt clever', we were at the top of the school and that meant (I came to realise) that we were in line for all sorts of honours. This sense of being exalted and slightly aloof from the girls in the 'lower ranks' was soon tempered when my English teacher described my handwriting to my mother (at a parents' evening) as 'looking like when a spider has dipped its legs into ink and walked across the page'!

I was an 'average' member of 1.1, excelling in music (as a result of private music lessons), English and history. In the fifth form I obtained seven 'O' levels, an average result. Careers' advice was an integral part of the fifth form programme and I recall that our history teacher was part of the careers team. The advice offered to me left me confused and unhappy. Why had she suggested that I go and work in Woolworths or in a sewing factory ('*like your mother had done*') when my friend who had got the same 'O' level results was advised to stay on to do 'A' levels?

The family discussed this advice and we all agreed that I should ignore it and follow my sister's footsteps. She had just passed her 'A' level Religious Studies in one year and got a grade B. This result was an indication of her determination. In the first year she had been placed in 1.3 and had worked her way out of this potential rut to become head of house (not sports captain) and to pass three 'A' levels. (She is now a barrister and a senior lecturer). I went on to take two 'A' levels and filled in a PCAS form as a matter of course, not really understanding the significance or the weight of the step. I remember the deputy head, Mrs Keeler helping me with the personal statement of the PCAS form.

Going to school and to church were the central activities in my life. My friends were church friends and my extended family were the 'brothers' and 'sisters' at church. Playing the piano for the church choir and the congregation, being a leader in the path-finders (a youth organisation like guides) gave me a sense of affirmation and optimism. As children and young people in the church, you had a range of adults taking a genuine interest in you. We were raised on sermons like 'Young, gifted and black' — a sideways look at our secular and spiritual position in British society, in conjunction with spiritual considerations. We learned, recited 'claimed' and believed bible promises like:

> Don't worry about anything; instead, pray about everything; tell God your needs and don't forget to thank him for his answers. Philippians 4:6.
>
> And it is he who will supply all your needs from his riches in glory, because of what Christ has done for us. Philippians 4:19.

> Even strong young lions sometimes go hungry, but those of us who reverence the Lord will never lack any good thing. Psalm 34:10.
>
> No one will be able to oppose you as long as you live, for I will be with you just as I was with Moses; I will not abandon you or fail to help you. Joshua 1:5.

We sang songs that told us about God's unconditional love for us and his willingness to assist us in all areas of our earthly life as well as providing a heavenly home, for example:

> Why should my heart be weary? Why should the shadows fall? Why should my heart be lonely and long for heaven and home? When Jesus is my portion my constant help is he, his eyes are on the sparrow and I know he watches over me (his eyes are on the sparrow, and I know he watches over me). I sing because I'm happy, I sing because I'm free, for his eyes is on the sparrow, and I know he watches over me.

I was sad to leave London but being offered a place at Sheffield Polytechnic felt like an achievement in itself! Leaving my family and friends would have been a daunting prospect if I did not know that there would be a 'church family' in Sheffield. My four years at the Poly, my subsequent return there as a senior lecturer and the current experience of writing this book leaves me with more questions than answers about the best strategies for surviving and thriving in a white male dominated racist education system.

In the following chapters I describe and discuss excerpts from the life histories of the respondents. My approach to, and understanding of their lives must be seen in the context of my own life history.

Chapter 4

Description of a range of themes

During and after the period of data collection I listened to the taped conversations. Similarities between the thought patterns, life experiences and areas of focus related by the respondents began to emerge as strong, important and highly relevant themes.

The subjects: a brief introduction

The population from which the sample was drawn for this study is small. Members of the African-Caribbean community in general and those belonging to the various churches were identified as possible subjects on the basis of their educational attainment. Where they had been educated was also significant. Those who had received all their education in the Caribbean before coming to England did not fit the criteria. The significant period of migration from the Caribbean meant that my subjects were likely to be between the ages of 25 and 40. To fit the criterion of an 'achiever', subjects had already to have obtained their first degree. In fact, over fifty percent of them had completed Masters courses, one had completed a doctoral thesis and two were pursuing their doctorates. Non-religious subjects were identified via Milroy's (1987) social networking system.

Certain statistical details are relevant. There are only two Seventh-Day Adventist Churches in Sheffield and the total membership does not exceed 300. Given that 99% of the membership is of African-Caribbean background, and the 1991 census registered only 8-10,000 African-Caribbeans in Sheffield, a city of 526,000, the promise of anonymity precludes the presentation of a great deal of personal detail. I interviewed twelve subjects but offer six pen pictures as examples of all twelve (quotes from all twelve will be used). The following pen pictures, with fictitious names, are therefore deliberately vague, as more specific details would almost certainly lead to the identification of the subjects.

Most of the subjects who took part in this study are or were resident in Sheffield at the time of the collection of data. All were aged between 25 and 45. Two-thirds were married and most had child-care responsibilities. Most of the subjects received all their education in England but a few had experienced differing lengths of primary and junior schooling in the Caribbean. All the subjects are currently in professional occupations in private or public settings, and a number hold senior positions in education establishments while others are at managerial level in various local authority departments.

Janet is about thirty years old. She has four siblings and received all her education in England. Her primary and junior and secondary schools were all in a multi-racial area but she was one of only two black girls in her secondary school, a grammar school. She failed her 'A' levels at the end of her sixth form and retook them at a technical college. Janet's four year degree prepared her to teach secondary school children. She currently holds a senior position in a school. She is an active member of her church.

Andrew did not arrive in England until he was twelve. His Caribbean education had been rigorous, if a little traditional. With his three siblings, he completed his schooling in England. His secondary school was a large inner city comprehensive with a high percentage of black pupils. He left school in the fifth form with few academic qualifications. However, Andrew took a series of part-time courses which finally earned him a first degree, quickly followed by a master's course and a principal level post in local government. Although he no longer attends church, Andrew continues to ensure that his children understand and appreciate Christian principles.

Jackie went to her local infant school. Her junior school was only a short bus ride away from home. In both these schools she recalls being verbally and physically abused because she was black. Because she was determined to defend herself, she was called 'a strong blackie'. Her four year degree course was an outstanding success and she obtained a first class degree. Jackie does feel that she has been discriminated against in the recruitment and selection process of employment. However, she is optimistic: she regards God as being in control of her life.

Jason is currently an active member of his church. Jason's parents came to England from the Caribbean but he and his brothers and sisters were all educated in England. His memories of school include consistently getting low marks, messing about with friends and 'rubbish careers advice' which reinforced the general message from his teacher. A message which implied that as adults these black pupils would never come to anything and would be the dropouts of society. Redundancy from a company in which he was employed in a manual capacity, in conjunction with other events in his life (e.g. becoming a youth leader at church), awakened in him a desire to improve himself. Success in Higher Education was not smooth but perseverance, confidence, prayer and community support got him through. All Jason's siblings are now employed in a professional capacity in a range of settings.

During the process of leaving the Caribbean, Kevin's parents spent a few years in the USA but finally decided to settle in the north of England. Education was a central theme in his home and the home of his cousins who lived nearby. There was even a sense of competition, as Kevin was honoured by the school with the position of head boy, while his cousin was 'only' a deputy head! Family attendance at church was interrupted because Kevin's mother was a nurse and worked irregular shifts. His father owned a small business and was not able to leave it for long periods. Kevin no longer attends church. He sympathises with aspects of the Rastafarian movement because it promotes notions of 'black pride'.

Joan's mother played a central role in her church and from an early age Joan was an integral part of the church. Her extended family networks and friendships were found among church members. However, church members seemed unwilling to address weighty socio-political questions that troubled Joan. Issues of power, inequality, social injustice and sexual relations were unconvincingly dealt with or presented as God's will. Some dissatisfaction with this lack of debate led Joan away from her church and to some extent away from Christianity. Joan received all her education in England and recalls her attitude as pro-learning but anti-school rules. She describes her University experience as enjoyable, although child care responsibilities hindered a leisurely approach to higher education.

The themes

The themes emerged during the process of the data collection and are grounded in the data (Glaser and Strauss, 1967). Many of the thematic headings, eg determination and resilience, were used by the subjects themselves to describe their experiences and their responses to them. In this chapter a range of themes spanning their school and home experiences are described and discussed, and quotes are offered to substantiate the subjects views on various areas. The themes are: school experiences, career guidance and advice, higher education, work experiences, racism, role models, family values and parental awareness and involvement. In the following chapter a similar format is used to explore the subjects' religious experiences and their affiliation with religious groups.

What follows are essentially descriptions of data from the life history subjects, arranged under a number of thematic headings. In their life histories they reflect on how they arrived at their professional positions, the role played by events, circumstances and other individuals in this process. In conversation, ideas flow from one notion to another. This fluid nature of gathering data inevitably results in the overlapping of the themes. The need for rigorous analysis of the data is not disputed; however, restricting the evaluation of the material by using an unsuitable mechanistic approach would fail to identify significant issues fully. (Whilst organisation according to themes is a useful way to handle the data, one has to continually bear in mind the fluid activity of the material and the fact that too rigid a categorisation may be counter-productive and may not enable fullest use of the data.) Obtaining an adequate balance between comprehension for the reader and presenting an authentic rendering of the subjects' news causes some tension. The differing merits of a range of research methods were fully discussed in Chapter three. Further exploration of these issues is presented in Chapter six, which focuses on the interpretation of the data.

Linguistic concerns

A number of researchers: Edwards (1979), Sutcliffe (1982) and others, have examined the linguistic experiences of black children. During the 1960s and 1970s language was considered a significant factor in the academic underachievement of black children (see Chapter one). Ironically, those respondents who were initially educated in the Caribbean found that their knowledge of English grammar was a strength on which they could build. Subjects were aware of the many cultural irrelevances that were central to the English curriculum being taught in the Caribbean. They were asked to relate to experiences and events that could not possibly have held any sense of reality for them. Andrew's personal experiences provide evidence which furthers this discussion.

Andrew had spent eleven enjoyable years in the Caribbean. English was his favourite subject at school and he was told by his teachers that he was good at it. He was not expecting the cultural conflict that occurred when he came to England. Communicating in English had never been a problem to him. Could this rejection of his language be a symbolic rejection of him? Elsewhere in his life history Andrew tells how his and his peers' enthusiasm for 'going to England' had been misinformed. No one had explained that their 'English' upbringing on a Caribbean island would not be accepted as 'good enough' in the 'mother country'. By rejecting their language, or at least their pronunciation, Britain was communicating its rejection of them as citizens. Andrew appeared ambivalent about how much he valued the education he had been offered in the Caribbean. On the one hand he valued its standards and quest for excellence, on the other hand he questioned the value and motivation of its Eurocentric approach.

In a particular class of his (English) junior school, a weekly oral spelling test was a regular feature. Andrew enjoyed this slot on the timetable as it gave him a chance to shine, although he found some other areas of the curriculum more difficult. The last person 'out' in this 'game' got a star or a prize! On one particular day Andrew's spelling was even better than usual. The teacher could not get him 'out'. Andrew felt proud. Then on a mere technicality, which turned out to be a cultural pronunciation difference, Andrew was 'out'. Andrew was sure that the teacher had been unfair and had deliberately undermined his self-esteem in front of his peer group. His classmates were laughing at him and the teacher looked triumphant! Andrew wondered whether the teacher would have done the same thing to a white boy in the class. Andrew described his experience as follows:

> It's inevitable, you know that you've been speaking the Queen's English for years in JA[1]. But the British teachers believe that you're going to have language problems! The kind of English problems I had was speaking English in an English/Sheffield way. I had to learn how to actually interpret things in books which were culture bound. That was a problem I had initially. I don't know how long it took me to get over that to clear that up. But there were a lot of frustrating things, like I told you about 'principle' and 'principal'. Problems that came because of the difference in pronunciation of words. In terms of reading I had no problems. I read avidly, I couldn't read enough and in terms of the structure of the English language and grammar and so on I was quite good on that 'cos I'd done a lot of work on that in JA. You know the English education is nowhere better than JA. For me that wasn't a problem, the grounding I had in JA in English Literature and English Language was sound. I was very good at English, ironically! That may be different from other people's experiences. It was more the cultural interpretation of the spoken word, rather than the written word and the read word.

Andrew continued,

> English was my strength. The reasons are quite clear. If you want a good English education you go to JA, where they are so steeped in colonialism that you get a 'more English' approach than 'the English give you over here'. I was reciting Shakespeare and Longfellow long before I ever came to this country. Talking about daffodils and snow, I had never seen them before! Luckily for me that slotted into some kind of reality when I came here. For others it could be difficult.

Janet's confidence about the status and use of language left her apparently unscathed, despite the negative social messages about Creole and her pronunciation. She had a rationale for understanding the socially constructed position of different languages, especially minority languages. What had given her this confidence when British society had communi-

1. Jamaica

cated many negative views about Caribbean languages? Indeed some of these negative perceptions have been internalised by some African-Caribbean people. A number of the life history subjects had evaluated the negative views they had encountered about their language and had concluded (possibly as a result of their social science education) that these views were overtly ethnocentric and covertly racist. During their primary, junior and secondary education, negative comments about their use of languages had never been contextualised within the framework of bilingualism. Corrections were made on the basis of incorrect English or carelessness. Janet discussed her experiences with languages:

> Dialect interference? No, I have had no mention of that, not since HE or after 'A' level. I know that in conversation I sometimes think in a patois mentality. Leaving S's off the ends of words etc., but when I am writing and I see the words down it's a different thing. I find it natural to use the correct grammar. Creole is part of my culture — I have aunts and uncles who speak broad Patois, but they hold official jobs. This dualism is quite natural. In Canada they have two languages. I give Creole the same status as being in a country where people are bilingual. I see myself as bilingual and if I make those so-called mistakes it's all in the eyes of the beholder. There's no difference for me if a French person living in England occasionally has problems with the pronunciation. A word may be influenced by the language or dialect, there's no difference. At school it was described as a handicap. But I point people to the Caribbean where I'm from, the education there is based on the British model but people can still speak as they feel comfortable. There is a case for focus and concentration on how and why you write and structure a sentence if written work is a problem.

Many African-Caribbeans in Britain regard their languages as a vehicle of identity and a means to power. Patois is regarded as a dynamic and versatile language to be used effectively in a range of settings. In their prayers, proverbs, lyrics, poems and novels, many African-Caribbeans find pride and relevance in the use of their language. Gillborn (1990) indicates how black children can use it in school as a challenge to white authority, a protest and a source of confidence and pride. The socio-linguistic and cultural aspects of the African-Caribbean language is discussed in Sutcliffe (1982).

African-Caribbean children are deemed to be handicapped in the English school system by their Creole background. Their use of standard English and vocabulary, pronunciation and grammar is often said to be corrupted by their Caribbean origins. Andrew's teacher appeared to believe that standard English was the only language through which education could be transmitted. Researchers (Coard, 1971, Edwards, 1979) have pointed out that British teachers' attitudes to Caribbean speech creates more problems for the child than does any area of language deficit. Racial and cultural awareness and sensitivity in these teachers would lead them to an understanding of the issues in terms of difference rather than deficit. Chapter one discussed the wider area of Creole and its status as a language.

Non-standard English speakers, including white working class children who speak a dialect are said to be deficient in their speech and therefore disadvantaged in their education. However, the middle class white child is considered to have all the qualities that are required for social advancement. Middle class speech, like standard English, is considered to be the norm and those who use these forms of communication are rewarded at school. There are, however, many different opinions about what is a language, or a 'dialect'? Partridge (1950) p.52 defines Standard English as: 'such English as is held to be proper and respectable, fitting and dignified...'

Quirk (1962) argues that:

> Standard English is basically an ideal mode of expression that we seek when we wish to communicate beyond our immediate community with members of the wider community and the nation as a whole, or with members of the still wider community (p.100).

These quotes indicate that most of the debates are based on social rather than linguistic factors. They have been challenged accordingly. Brandt (1984), for example, makes a distinction between Caribbean Creole, Creole as it is and was spoken in the Caribbean, British Caribbean Creole, the form of Creole spoken in England and British Youth Caribbean Creole, the form of Creole spoken in England by a group of black (and some white) youth. He argues that Caribbean Creole is a distinct language of polygenetic origin that has regenerated itself over the centuries. He further states that young black people have attributed to Creole a special and political resistance; resistance to the racial oppression and cultural dominance of white society. Brandt argues for the incorporation of the mother tongue in the education of young black pupils as there is some evidence for the use of Black Youth Caribbean Creole as a part of black youth's own anti-racist struggle.

A number of the respondents commented on the extent to which they valued the Caribbean language. It provided a sense of pride and belonging, as they struggled to maintain a sense of dignity. Indeed, some respondents used their Caribbean language at school with other black friends, to the frustration of both white peers and white teachers. Using it allowed areas of their lives to be kept private and safe from white intervention. However, the incorporation of Caribbean languages into the British school curriculum was a controversial issue. Respondents felt that white teachers were unable to teach the subject. Specialist teachers were seen as a possible way forward but a number of the subjects feared that their language could be laid open to ridicule while still being marginalised.

School experiences

Joan's mother had selected a school in the nicer part of town, as she felt that it was better resourced and had a better reputation than those in the inner city. Although a comprehensive at the time she attended, her school was living on an outdated reputation based on its previous status as a grammar school. Joan was one of few black children there.

The following incident occurred during her first or second year in school. Needlework classes, unlike games sessions, are peaceful, with the minimum of noise or even chatter. An unsolicited public lecture in zoology and botany was offered in full view and hearing of all her classmates and with very little appreciation for the feelings of the two girls involved. A number of assumptions informed the teacher's apparent need to give this lecture. She assumed that she knew where the girls lived and indicated that she had some knowledge about the urban rather than rural nature of their neighbourhood.

> We were doing needlework and the teacher called us over. The school, by the way, is located in a beautiful part of Rusville. It used to be a grammar school. I remember the teacher calling me and this other black girl over to draw our attention to this tree with birds in it. 'Come

> over here Joan and Julie', she said. 'There are some birds in that tree, I don't suppose you see many birds or trees in Naling', (the area we lived in, where a lot of black people lived). That teacher was making a comment about where we lived. Basically by inviting us to look at the birds and the tree she was saying that we lived in the ghetto, the run down area of the city — which it wasn't, at that time. She had no clue about it! She was making a comment about where we lived and our experiences, a negative one. There were other things of that nature. That stands out particularly because of the attitude that came over and what she was saying and the other kids laughing. It was a negative point that she was making.

Embarrassment was the mildest of the emotions Joan experienced at the time. A sense of unbelonging and alienation overwhelmed both girls. Like Andrew, they felt belittled and grossly undermined. It was not a comment about their abilities or lack of ability, but a damning comment about their families, their communities and their living standards. Should they not have challenged the teacher's assumptions and insensitive attitude? They obviously felt that this would have been unwise. The teacher was oblivious to the girls' feelings. The white pupils were amused. When the lesson was finished the two black girls might have discussed the incident; it would certainly have thrown them together as victims of oppression. The extent to which they discussed it might depend on how well they knew each other and how well each knew the other's views on racism.

Jackie's mother had few options in choosing her daughter's school. She had no car to transport Jackie to a primary or junior school where her child could possibly have been better prepared and have had a chance to pass the 11+. It could be that most black children failed the 11+ because of the poor preparation in the ill-equipped primary and junior schools they attended. In the following quotation, Jackie reflects on the limited opportunities, the 'prewritten education and career script' prepared for her. In other parts of her life history she ponders upon what factors sustained a sense of motivation and determination to break out of the limited and stereotypical set of expectations the school had for her and other black girls.

Throughout her account we get a sense of how she has subsequently considered her own position (through social science perceptions) and also how she has tried to understand the position and experiences of the teachers. With low standards in some inner city schools it could be that these teachers felt trapped too. They too had few options; their morale was low. Jackie reflects on the process of her school experience:

> In terms of my formal education I went to the local primary and junior school. I failed the 11+, as did most other black children of my age. I went to a secondary modern all girls school where (I think there is evidence to support this) the teachers had 4 or 5 'O' levels themselves. The National Curriculum may be a good thing because it wasn't until I left school and went to FE college that I experienced certain aspects of science.
>
> It was the year CSEs were introduced. I got a few CSE grade 2s and one grade 1. The fact that I am in this job today contradicts and eradicates the deficiency theories and the psychology about set intelligence and inability. These theories suggest that if intelligence is not revealed at an early stage of development then it doesn't exist. I think part of my problem was to do with the actual school itself. The teachers were not academically capable of providing basic education, never mind anything else, and how we got through CSEs with relatively high grades, I don't know. When I left school at 16 I still had this burning ambition to achieve something, but the expectations the school had for us were as follows (when I think of the hidden curriculum and the formal curriculum): it was about providing potential shop assistants, factory workers etc., unskilled, semi-skilled posts.

Other respondents reflected on the negative nature of their British school experience, and on time spent in the Caribbean. Nick's ambivalence about his Caribbean educational experience was similar to Andrew's. On the one hand Nick appears to value this primary socialisation which provided him with positive role models of black people. It was less likely for him to internalise inferior, racist or oppressive views of black people than it is for young black people born and brought up in England. He said, 'Luckily I was brought up on an island where black people were in the majority. I saw them doing all sorts of different jobs.'

Those role models were reinforced over time, as he had many vacations in the Caribbean: 'I was going back regularly at one time, the family went nearly every summer'.

On the other hand Nick was critical of the disciplinarian approaches in Jamaican schools during his father's early education:

> My education was better than my father's experience. If he put his hand up in class and got the answer wrong he got beaten. Those who didn't put their hands up to answer any questions got beaten as well. A real catch 22 situation!

The use of physical punishment was obviously abhorrent to Nick. Caning and other forms of corporal punishment have for a number of years been frowned on in the British education system. Nick had obviously internalised these British values about the rights of children and notions of self-determination in education.

Nick spent the first eight years of his life in JA. When he arrived in England the school system did not adequately assess his academic abilities. Nick explains:

> I came to England in 1966, when streaming was still operating openly. I was put in the bottom stream. Fortunately I didn't stay there for very long. I moved up into the top streams. I think a lot of that progress was down to a particular teacher. We had form teachers, she was a white lady and lived quite near my parents. She spent a lot of time with me. I remember being in the bottom stream although I was 8 or 9. The teacher asked these easy questions and I could answer all of them. The other children were flicking things about. The teacher seemed to view teaching as a chore rather than an enjoyable task. There weren't many other black children around. We didn't get into double figures. I stopped in the top stream. The top stream didn't take the 11+. Instead we took an entrance exam for the local grammar school. Most of the people in my class went to the grammar schools. I went to one of these single sex grammar schools for boys.

Having had the apparent academic advantage of starting school at three and a half years old in the Caribbean, Nick was still assessed as being educationally well below average for his age group when he came to England. Research which highlights the systematic misassessment of black children's educational ability (Coard, 1971) relates Nick's experience to a wider debate.

It is evident from Nick's account that he was frustrated in a class of children who were low achievers. His Caribbean educational experience would have taught him to behave in a quiet, respectful manner in school. Like other life history subjects who began their schooling in the Caribbean and continued it in England, the disrespectful, ill-mannered behaviour of their English peers was at first overwhelming.

Why did this one teacher devote her time and effort to assist this particular child? How did Nick and his family experience her overtures? A sense of mistrust is a common response from black families (community members) when white professionals appear to become personally involved, offering help outside of their institutional and role.

Nick and his parents were grateful that his teacher discerned his academic abilities and potential and was willing to steer him through the system. They were 'outsiders', not knowing how best to tackle the system. A number of the life history subjects recalled the patronising, evasive attitude of many teachers. As parents themselves, the life history subjects could draw on their own parents' experiences and felt more able to tackle the most difficult areas of parent/teacher communication.

In my conversations with Joan and Andrew they shared with me a number of recent events which they felt demonstrated that the teachers could be less than forthcoming about their children's educational progress. Joan recalls:

> I went to parents' evenings. My son's maths teacher kept saying what a nice helpful boy he was. I pointed out that I was pleased to hear that but was equally interested in his progress in maths. She stuttered a bit and then said he was trying hard but had some difficulties. I really had to push her to 'spell out' what the difficulties were.

Similarly Andrew's daughter's form teacher commented at length on her outstanding sporting ability. He (the teacher) needed prompting to focus the discussion on educational matters. It transpired that Andrew's daughter had not been progressing satisfactory during the past two terms. Andrew recalls:

> I had to point out that as parents we expected to be kept in touch about our child's progress. I had to initiate a system, through which we regularly monitored her school work.

Many respondents and their parents became familiar with the need to challenge institutions. So the respondents recall being surprised when white people were helpful to them.

For whatever reason, Nick's teacher worked with him and helped to guide him out of the potential educational wilderness, 'the remedial class'. Nick obviously belonged in the top stream, because once he got there, he stayed there, and he was successful in his entrance exam for a grammar school. Would Nick and his parents have been able to challenge the education system without the help of that teacher? Can the personal attempts of white individuals working in an anti-racist fashion in a racist public institution make significant impact? These questions raise extremely important issues which can only be flagged up in this study. To unravel these questions would require another book.

From this and other experiences, Nick has developed on open philosophy which enables him to forge close and sometimes intimate relationships with white people. A number of the respondents felt similarly.

Sports and black children in schools

The attraction of, or steering of, large numbers of African-Caribbean young people to participating in extra-curricular sporting activities has caused much heart-searching and distress in black families. A number of publications correctly outline the anxieties of many black families:

> Turning to prospects beyond school, conspicuous symbols of black success, Viv Richards, Frank Bruno, Daley Thompson, will hold a particular cultural significance for young working-class black males who will seek in top-level sport, success and approbation as an alternative to the stigmatised status accorded to blacks. Others will take up sport to try and enhance their material and social status.
>
> These factors may help to explain why African-Caribbean males are more highly motivated than other groups towards achievement in sports... few will succeed in entering sports... and even fewer will make more than a decent living from it for a brief part of their working lives. For the vast majority, the dream of upward mobility through sport can never become a reality. In this respect sport can be regarded as a sedative, a stultifying force, reinforcing the marginal position of Afro-Caribbeans in society (Carrington, 1986, p.103).

Janet was unsure about the impact that excessive involvement with sports had on the academic achievement of her siblings, but thought that it might have been a hindrance to her sisters. She was more certain about the negative impact it had on her brother's school career. Yet, maybe subconsciously, she knew that being good at sports was a sure way to receive 'positive strokes' from the school establishment. Janet 'joked' about this aspect of her own school life. We can only speculate on whether at the time she wished she had the sporting skills that could have brought her affirmation. In the following, she ponders on the important role sport often plays for black children:

> Sports? No! I was hopeless, a lot of the black girls were good. The ones who were held in high esteem were the athletes. But it was not my potential for greatness! My brother and sisters were very good. I don't know what went wrong with me! (Laugh) Yes when I go home I look at their old school photographs and medals that they keep at school and home. They were good at academics as well. Yet some were held back — put in CSEs instead of GSE's etc. My brother was good at football. I'm sure he suffered academically because of it. He's quite a timid person. My sisters were good at netball and running but they have all done very well academically. Were they 'good' at sports or were they nurtured and encouraged into sports? That's the question! They were noticed as being good from the junior school. My brother maybe suffered most, as there are few role models other than music or sports for black boys in Britain, in general.

Racism

Racism has profound psychological and social impact on the lives of black people in Britain. It often leaves the person, especially young people who are emotionally seeking for messages of approval as a means to develop independence and self-actualisation, doubting their value to society and their purpose in life. Because of the prevalence of negative messages, black individuals may choose to resist and challenge societal pressures; this reaction often attracts accusations of being paranoid and or 'having a chip on their shoulder'. This 'victim blaming' approach only isolates the person further, resulting in different and more intense forms of resistance. In the following passages the respondents reflect on incidents they identify as evidence that racism has had some impact on their lives, and on the general impact of racism on the lives of their community. Here Janet vividly describes her feelings about the impact of racism:

> The thing with me, I think, is that I was brought up to believe not by my family but by the school and the society that very little was expected of me. I have nothing to say that anybody would possibly be interested in. I have nothing to contribute. I am made to feel that to a certain extent in this place (work setting) there's a special place for me in this society and it's at the bottom. What I find incredibly debilitating (this is part of the confidence problem), I find myself quite often stopping and pinching myself. There's me out there, a black girl, worthless, of little importance, of little consequence. And there's this person here holding a very responsible position making crucial decisions — about people's lives. At times I can't make the connections, because it's like living through a dream. I don't think about it much but it's very debilitating. I think that these feelings about myself, lacking self-worth, or expectations, can be a stumbling block. You're in a position of psyching yourself sometimes. Most white colleagues do not come from a background such as mine. Rather they are coached. It is almost a natural progression. They are often invited to apply for posts such as these. Sensitive is the wrong word but feeling that you don't belong. Being told that by one's colleagues directly or indirectly is very debilitating, very disconcerting. I still feel very hurt, to the extent I feel tearful when I think of what people do.

When those who left the Caribbean in the 1950s and 60s faced overt racism and discrimination, they coped with it, hoping that their children would have a better experience. Janet's remarks suggest that this hope was in vain. In an attempt to provide and sustain family and community support, many Caribbeans lived in close proximity. Material and moral support between community members was important, since wider society was oppressive.

The pain and hurt expressed by Janet is often echoed by black individuals who live in Britain. At other times they objectively identify the process, intention and consequences of racism. They do not always 'wallow' in despair. Various strategies are harnessed as possible responses. 'Over-reacting' to 'prove' your worth, refusing to join the 'rat race', opting out of society's expectations are just a few possible responses; others might be direct challenges as described earlier. A number of the respondents chose to ignore racist behaviour or comments, treating with deserved contempt the perpetrators of these injustices. Andrew was philosophical about the possible range of responses:

> I know that I am not being paranoid, it's been happening all my life. You notice it all the time, and it depends what sort of mood you're in, you either ignore it or make a point of it. Most of the time you ignore it cause you're so used to it. Because I haven't got an obvious West Indian name, not a Delroy or Errol or Winston, and because of my accent, people don't perceive me as black. Its always good to see people's reaction. For example when welcomed to the Grammar School it was: Welcome.... I'm sure you'll be an excellent member of the sports team. My father had dealings with many people who were told: We don't think you'll pass the 'O' level but try the CSE. To a child and his parents not aware of the British system it may seem reasonable. But most people know that not even a CSE 1 is treated in the same way as an 'O' level grade C or D or whatever.

Given the regular problem of racism, individual benevolence of white individuals was not expected. Rita remembers the interest and kindness of her first employer, a white woman:

> She wished me well, said it was the best thing I could do because she thought I was a bright person. It was extraordinary because never before had a white person shown such interest. At that stage I couldn't articulate these experiences in terms of racism. She thought good of me and had good expectations of me. She would say 'oh that's good', 'you are good', 'I wish I could do that', I found it extraordinary. Although I went off to college she understood the financial situation and she offered me a Saturday job.

Other offers of help from white colleagues seemed less genuine. Indeed the motivation of the offer was not always obvious. After an open disagreement with the headmaster at his school, Kevin obtained an interview for a post in another school. It seemed completely out of character when his current headmaster offered him a 'dummy interview'. Kevin was not sure of his motive but given the relationship he had with this man, any 'offer of help' was regarded with suspicion. Why should his line manager want to help Kevin, especially when he has made it clear that Kevin was 'way out of his league' in applying for the job?

Kevin recalls:

> 'I don't think you have much chance', he said, 'but you've got an interview so I'll give you a dummy interview'. I didn't want to do it but I thought it might be useful, so I went round to his house at night for this dummy interview. I couldn't believe it 'Oh come in' he said really abruptly. He took me into this room. He was sat behind a desk. I was sat there for ages — he deliberately went out to upset me. Then he asked me these irrelevant questions. After ten minutes I got really annoyed and angry and my answers to the questions became monosyllabic. When he had finished he said 'let's go for a drink'. He said 'Had that been the real situation you wouldn't have got the job'. I said 'yes, I know and do you know why?' He felt it was the sort of situation I'd have to deal with in the real interview. But with real human beings I walked it. I heard I interviewed very well. So I got the job there and for me it was a real turning point.

Research projects and other modes of investigation have without exception documented the impact of racism on the past and present socio-economic position of African-Caribbean people in Britain. Poor working hours, low wages and few opportunities all have a serious impact on the extent to which parents could monitor their children's school experiences, liaise with teachers or offer supplementary assistance at home. Access to knowledge about the best way to use the school system was not always available to black parents. Jason reflects on the possible impact of his family's socio-economic position and how this might have had differing effects on older and younger siblings:

> It could be because I was the youngest and the family had more time to establish themselves economically here because in common with a lot of black people they struggled when they came here. My father worked shifts, my mother worked as well every hour God sent, they needed every penny. Maybe it was because I wasn't old enough to work, but my bigger sister was old enough to work when we arrived in England. The teacher told my parents about the capabilities of my little sister and they told her: rubbish. The girl was really bright. She

> was reading at that stage. They assumed the wrong things and they put you in the wrong form, won't enter you for exams. These things worked against them. It could be economic factors, more time for them to establish themselves in the country, that saved me.

Kevin was concerned about his own negative experience in schools but he was equally bewildered about his siblings' experiences. He regards his position as a lucky escape from possible disaster. Kevin suggests that his parents were marginally more prepared to deal with the education system because they had been through it with his older sister. Adjusting to a new country, finding employment in an inflexible work situation, left little time and space for Kevin's parents to be creative or systematic with their children's education. It appears that the family's socio-economic position and the impact of racism were directly related to the children's school experience.

Role models

With a lack of obvious public role models, the life history subjects found their inspiration from a range of sources, some political and others recreational. Whatever the source, they 'used' these role models to validate their experiences as worthwhile people. The role models helped to boost their self-esteem.

> You'd have to look very hard in the 60s and early 70s for black role models. When I was at school, eg secondary school, grammar school in particular, there weren't any role models. I was the only black face within the system and there weren't any role models I knew in this society.

Family members were often identified as role models, in that they had previously achieved what were considered to be good jobs. The daily grind of dealing with racism in educational institutions and employment situations had to be undertaken without regular affirmation that black people were succeeding, despite individual and institutional oppression. As the respondents reflect on the current growth of black people in professional settings, there is a sense of mild optimism. Kevin again:

> The only person who was a target in that way was my brother and the interest and drive that black parents have in their kids' education. My

brother achieved quite highly in JA. He was the academic. He had a good job etc. that was a spur because he had done it, all that time ago. I think it was particularly difficult for black people at that time, for the system was only just recognising that black people were capable of being teachers, that was a real problem. I was a real loner at school and the Poly. There were people in the community I had come of age with, but they tended to be either peers or a little older, rather than role models in that sense. I think it's later on when I look around at black people in the system, I think yea! it's great. It's a good feeling. Back then, there wasn't a black face in the system.

Much of my progress was down to parental pressure. A lot of my uncles were encouraged at school. My godfather was the first black magistrate in the city where we lived. He was considered bright in Barbados, he went to a decent school there. When he came here he ended up in a factory doing some menial job. Then he went to night school for qualifications and went on to be a tax inspector, civil servant, senior tax inspector, then the first black mayor. He was all the time talking to me and encouraging me.

My father drives a lorry. He's been self-employed for a long time, he's got his own business. When I reflect on it, what he did was a remarkable achievement. He set up a small business which has been very successful, and achieved a great deal under very difficult circumstances.

Family values

An intense sense of gratitude and appreciation was expressed by the respondents for the environment provided in their homes. They now recalled with adult perceptions the values which were shared in their families. Much of this philosophy and underlying value system was unspoken but it sent a powerful message to the youth in these homes. Rita said:

When you get older you reflect. I think about my father's own achievements against the odds. This must have had some influence on all of us. It was an urge, a need to succeed. My mother was a nursing assistant. She came from a middle class family in Jamaica but she didn't get much education as she was the eldest and looked after the

> others. Her brothers and sisters are local government officers and doctors in the USA. Understandably she had an ambivalent attitude towards us stopping on at school.
>
> She wanted us all to get a good education and 'go high' as she would say. But there were also financial pressures. If we had gone out to work we could have helped. But we all stayed on at school in the end till 18. She wanted us to have the opportunity of doing what she would have liked to do.
>
> I don't know whether I should say this but my mother can only barely read and write. When I think of that woman from the time she came to this country she's worked and organised the family. OK, I was sometimes the substitute mother but I was still relying on her organisation. I think if she was only given the opportunity. The woman can plan and organise. Just imagine how many balls she had to juggle at once. We never went to school dirty.

Rita radiated a sense of pride and admiration as she gave credit to the parenting approach of her mother and father. She admitted that some of what she now regards as influencing factors subconsciously informed her behaviour as a child. Her parents' options were limited but they always chose what was in the best interests of their children. With hindsight, Rita struggled to find words to express her appreciation and bewilderment at how her parents coped in such difficult times. She said:

> I've got to say I admire them and it's to their credit to a large extent that we've succeeded the way we have. There are important family factors to do with my background which have some influence on my attainment.

Typically for the life history subjects, education played a central role in all their homes. It was the opposite of the peripheral role it is said to play in white working class homes. Parent involvement in education emerges in more depth in other parts of the conversations. Subjects were aware of the significant role of education. Nick recalled his own experiences:

> I don't think that it is unusual for most black families. I know in that era it was a continuation of what you learnt and was bred into you in JA. 'You go to school to learn boy'. If you get trouble at school with the teacher you better not say anything at home or you got double

> beating. From that perspective there was a lot wrong with the education system in JA — the corporal punishment aspect. But the child-rearing messages were 'You go to school to learn. Whatever the teacher does she is right. If you're doing something wrong, you're getting a beating, it's you're fault'. The same thing carried on over here. Black people who came here were innocent. They came across not believing that people can be racist. Because if you were going to hate a neighbour you had a reason for it. They couldn't believe that people hated you for your colour. That line of reasoning was translated into educational practices etc. If you go to school even in this country you say and do what the teacher wants and whatever mark the teacher gives you is the mark you deserve. That was the clear message. It took a long time for people like my parents to realise that teachers could mark down 'cos you black. In terms of education the message from home was 'You go there you learn. You keep you head down'.

Many of the respondents reported how they felt 'torn' between home values and school values. Whereas excellence in education was regarded as of utmost importance at home, mediocrity was accepted as the norm at school. Beyond that, many felt that attempting to attain a standard of excellence was well nigh impossible in a racist environment.

For a number of years members of black (including Asian) communities have registered their dismay and resentment at the conclusions (mainly) white middle class male sociologists have drawn about the lifestyles and values held by their communities. Nick wanted to set the record straight in the light of his own experience.

> In terms of the child-rearing practices our family was typical of other black families. You obey your parents. There must be respect. The kind of things you can and can't say... the code was quite clear. I can say this to you but not to many white people because they don't understand what's going on. Laying down standards was important. For which we're all very grateful. We were all treated equal. If there was a sexist thing in the family it wasn't overt. I'd make fire same as my sister. I'd wash dishes same as my sister. I happen to like sewing so if we were making cushions we'd all work together. I'm telling you! Singing with your family in different harmonies. We make sorrel, bread and bun at Easter. The family life was full. You took part

> in everything. My sisters did the cooking, but we tended to do things together. In that way we were a unit and the lads were very close as well.

Nick was aware and conscious of the negative stereotyping that has pathologised black families in Britain. The cohesion, warmth and devotion that he describes is rarely explored in British sociological literature. He argued that the demands made of children with respect to education and other standards need to be discussed within this framework. He continued:

> Well, nobody likes beating. Sometimes you 'bex' till you could almost commit murder. But with all that there's the caring structure. Things you do together, like family outings. When I was 18 and we used to always get lost driving around in Manchester. We used to holiday together, cook and sit down and tell jokes. Your parents would start telling anecdotes about their life. I miss that. There were always good times. We shared in everything. When things were plenty, you got. When things were tight you all shared. Things like even buying clothes. Whose turn it was for large items and everybody got something. The family structure and discipline was important and by white standards at times it may seem harsh. But it was within the JA tradition and expectation and with all that there is a lot of love and support. The discipline and structure tells you that you are in a society that doesn't treat you fair. You have to be clear about who you are and where you are going and what the rules of the game are.

The examination of British African-Caribbean family culture from the viewpoint of the subjects has not been successfully explored.

As a community, black individuals are often seen as a homogeneous group who belong to the working or underclasses. Mass media foster and nurture this impression. The attempts by individual black people to aspire to middle class values in Britain have received little positive examination by mainstream sociologists. Nick identified issues which deserve further exploration.

> In JA my father was a baker. My mother was a cook in a hotel in JA. They were upper working class aspiring towards middle class status. They always saw education as being very important and they saw it

> as a way that their kids could be better than they were. The socio-economic structure of society in JA was different from what it is over here. The fact that my father was a baker and had work regularly and my mother was a cook and had that job umpteen years gave them some kind of status which that occupation wouldn't have over here. Manual work is valued in a much more meaningful way than it is over here. They suffered and sacrificed a lot to make sure that we had a good education and that paid off. When they came here they still had a positive feeling about education. So they were working class and or if there's an upper W.C. they aspired to middle class ideas about education, life etc. I saw them as somewhere in that category. They in fact wanted all the kids to get the best out of education — it was important for all the kids.

If these socio-economic factors and the aspirations of black families were as fully examined as negative stereotypes, the education and sociological literature might take account of the extent to which educational aspirations have been suppressed in black children. Writers in these areas need to comment on British school values about succeeding, and the extent to which striving for the best is often destroyed or nullified. The following explores black parents' attempts to sustain and revitalise these values.

Parental involvement/awareness

We have already noted how parents often did not have detailed knowledge about the education system. The sort of knowledge that comes via an informal network was not available to them. However, even with limited knowledge and experience of the education system they used options and made decisions about their children's school career. In some cases these decisions demanded a great deal of sacrifice on their part. Angela said:

> I was reflecting on school experiences. I remember the school that I was at. My parents had used their options of Sec Mod school. My mother said: 'You not going to P.T. girl school and mixing with those other black children — before long you won't be taking any notice of your lessons. You're going to another school where you'll get something in your head.' When I think about it my mother sent me four miles across town to the best of the all Secondary Mods. Even

> though it was so pathetic as I said. In the school there were about 400 girls and out of that 400 there were five black girls.

Angela's mother could be accused of being 'racist to her own'. By refusing to allow her daughter to go to a certain school, was Angela's mother implying that she was 'better than' other black people who lived in the same catchment area? On the contrary, Mrs T was aware that the poor reputation of the local school was not the children's fault. She knew that if her child attended that school the same fate (i.e. low grades, few exam results, poor employment opportunities) awaited her. However, children are less discerning (see Chapter three for my own choices). When Angela was in the fourth year of junior school she had planned with her friends what they would do in their Secondary School, and social activities were the children's main concern. They had heard that the school had a good netball team, and several of them knew they would make the team. Angela was disappointed at her mother's decision. Making new friends in 'that' school might be difficult. To date Angela's experience with most white people had been distant. Yes, she did have a few white 'friends' at school. But they didn't mix much outside of school. To her, most white people were aloof and the thought of being isolated on their territory was unattractive.

Few of the families represented by the respondents were financially 'well off'. The temptation to allow or encourage the youth in the family to contribute to the housekeeping budget by leaving school at the earliest opportunity, appears to have been an issue. Sometimes this was discussed openly; on other occasions they could read between the lines and identify their parents' passion for education. Rita recalls her parents' position:

> My mother, although she didn't say it to me at the time, was torn between the eldest child going out and getting a bit of money. But after I got the job she said, 'I don't want you to continue shop work. I want you to go and get an education, no shop work.' For me it was difficult — I had a bit of money coming in, I could buy things, I really didn't want to leave the job. I can remember my mother saying, 'It's either you pack up the shop work or you can take your things, take your money and get out of this house'. I left school in June, started the job in July and by September that year I was at the local FE college.

The importance of education was a common theme in the lives of all the subjects. Many of these parents played an active role, visiting schools, monitoring their children's work, maintaining a systematic 'programme' at home which was aimed at maximising their children's academic potential. Positive and negative incentives were used to ensure that children ordered their priorities. Knowing about the views of white teachers about black people's sporting ability, parents were often keeping a tight reign on this avenue of school activities. Joan's parents were clear about their daughter's career progress:

> As soon as I'd done the 'O' level it was you're doing 'A's. I wanted to anyway but it was certainly encouraged. If not both, at least one of my parents attended the PTA meetings. They were there as soon as the school was opened. They gave the teachers the Spanish inquisition. They spent time reading my report and looking at my homework. They didn't always understand it but they'd look at my marks and if they were going in the wrong direction various measures were taken to influence me to get them going the other way. To some people it may seem a hard, callous upbringing but there was a lot of love around in all that. It was tough and hard but I knew my parents loved me. There was plenty of support and affection there. I was brought up between two sets of grandparents. I remember being sat down every Sunday and made to go through my times tables and if I got it wrong — SLAP. It was a very Victorian approach to education in terms of that. But it did me good. I was reading and writing and able to do simple arithmetic before most people. It was very structured, very strict. My parents were aware of certain things, they insisted that I did my academic work first. I was good at a few sports, but if my marks were low I couldn't play for the team even if I was picked.

Bagley et al (1978) (see Chapter one) refer to the authoritarian approach to child-rearing by Jamaican parents. They conclude that this 'cultural lag' of styles of discipline is a significant factor in the 'generation gap' between black youths and their parents. This pathological view of the Caribbean family neglects significant factors raised by Joan. Black parents, as represented by Joan's mother choosing a firm approach to child-rearing, should not be viewed as politically passive immigrants who seek to contain and control their children through physical punishment. Similarly, strategies adopted by black youths cannot simply be seen as a reaction to or rebellion against their parents' values and approaches. Bagley observes that:

> Today such parental values are no longer functional and indeed create considerable problems when black teenagers, influenced by the standards of their white peers, may in consequence rebel at the structures and passive conservatism of their parents as they recruit themselves into ideological positions which are highly critical of English society (p.76).

Such a view divides the generations into 'passive' and 'active' categories. Older people are seen as passive and content to accept their position in British society, while black youths are viewed as suffering from 'culture-clash', alienated and therefore in need of intervention by the state. The black parents of these subjects were part of the earlier campaigns of the 'right to stay in Britain' or campaigners against 'Educational Subnormal placements and sin-bins'. They may also have been involved in the struggles for self-determination on the international front (eg independence movements) as well as the daily struggle of bringing up children and keeping families intact, amid growing hostility in this country (Patel, 1990).

Knowing that they were actively excluded from any local institution which would formally or informally inform them of their rights and options as local citizens, individuals in the black community were often proactive in setting up such organisations within which they could help themselves and each other. Financial assistance and information sharing were the hallmarks of these organisations. Kevin spoke about his dad's involvement in community groups:

> Although I said we lived in a white area, my dad was very active in the black community. He and a couple of cousins set up a black members club which is still going. It gives loans for redeveloping buildings, organising discussions about aspects of their lives like sickle cell disease, education for their children and housing problems.

Unlike authors such as Bagley, the subjects understood and appreciated their parents' actions. Andrew recalls:

> I had this typical West Indian upbringing which was strict. I had to always let my parents know where I was. Always take off my uniform as soon as I got home, go and do my homework. No sitting by the TV — straight to my books, straight to my room. I didn't really resent any of it cos I didn't know any different. I had always had that sort of thing, in fact my parents had to stop me from reading. I was the 'typical' torch-under-the-bed-sheets kind of child (to read books). I read anything, not just any particular subjects, anything at all. I enjoyed school, I used to win a few prizes. But never have a mother who is a nurse — she had no compassion whatsoever. I was sent to school many times with colds, no sympathy (laugh). People were kept off with snuffs or coughs, not me. I hardly missed a day. I always won the attendance prize!

Higher Education

Negative school experiences were often repeated and aggravated in higher education. Predominantly white, middle class, male university and polytechnic lecturers frequently reacted with some surprise at the presence of black students. This reaction caused some questioning and anxiety for the often 'lonely' black student. Contact with assessors are usually strained, with a typically adversarial relationships between student and lecturer. The interaction with the respondents' peers was not markedly better. Increasing reports (e.g. Melkie, 1990) confirm that African-Caribbean students are producing lower results than their white peers and many are leaving courses before they have completed the whole programme. Rita reflects on her negative experience in higher education:

> When I was there in 1978, I hated my degree because it wasn't what I wanted. I was a phenomenon — the first and only Black African-Caribbean woman in the department. Racism. Yes, there was racism on the part of the lecturers in a subtle way. I found the experience with the students in my year (there were 120 of us) quite harrowing for a number of reasons. Race was part of it, but the snobbery I found most difficult and harrowing. It was the 'class' factor. Apparently there's a tradition there, if you don't get in to read at Oxford, the next place to try is M, because of their expertise in my subject. A lot of the students were from public schools and for the vast majority of the students

> university was a natural progression. It was not for me; I sometimes wondered why I was there. I couldn't relate. Many of the students were very wealthy, they had cars and were able to buy a house. Their parents could come to pick them up at the end of term in their BMW or Rolls Royce. I had very little in common with them! I got a class of degree which made me angry. It was a blow to my confidence. It's only just picked up, just about. I'm convinced; and I met a couple of radical lecturers, who were there at the time. They said I should have got a better class of degree. What was against me was my attitude to the course. I wasn't putting the arguments over the way they wanted. In retrospect, I now know that my approach was the right one. I was using some of my experiences, with the theory.

In that lengthy account, Rita raises many different issues which require further discussion.

Feelings of embarrassment and alienation, described by Andrew and Joan as they recalled their school experiences, were familiar to Rita during her four years at University. Social/psychological concepts of the need to belong could be used here to unpack Rita's experience. She was not allowed to be a member of the group — both her peers and teachers made it clear that she was outside the 'norm'.

> They were constantly 'gob smacked' by me. It was very much an experience of not listening to what I was saying but looking at me (my physical presence).

During the 1980s, Racism Awareness Training courses were used to point out to white people the nature and impact of their racist behaviour. However in 1978, before these courses were popular and elements of them incorporated into many social science courses, Rita embarked on her degree. White liberal individuals could be patronising or even offensive without feeling any guilt. Rita experienced their behaviour as offensive. Yet, many white individuals may argue that much of the behaviour interpreted as racist is only a white person's way of trying to befriend. Such line of argument and set of expectations often caused the black students to doubt themselves. The 'class' dimension seemed to be of real significance for Rita. She felt that her colour and socio-economic position excluded her from the 'in group'. It is interesting to speculate whether the class factor was more significant than race. Would she have felt as excluded if she had been financially equal to the other students? These issues deserve further examination but that examination cannot be undertaken in this book.

The final results of her four year degree felt as unsatisfactory as her time spent there. Was Rita unrealistic about her academic abilities? Why was she angry about the final result? Why did it come as a surprise to her? Was she unfamiliar with the processes by which the 'class' of degree would be decided?

A number of the respondents spoke about the extent to which they felt they were 'under-marked' in further and higher education. This suspicion was more keenly felt when these individuals had written assignments concerned with the issue of racism. Comments from tutors suggested that they found the students' work insufficiently academic. Lecturers noted that elements of subjectivity marred exploration which needed objective examination. Often social science students had been attracted to the study of the area of racism because they regarded it to be relevant to their daily experience. However the sharing of their personal experiences in the context of academic exploration often appears to be problematic.

When Rita refers to her 'attitude to the course', it brings to mind the 'Paul Dixons' and other characters in Gillborn's study (1990). Those who had 'survived' and 'succeeded' had chosen a less confrontational stance. Students who chose to assert themselves and their views were 'punished' though various institutional processes. As Gillborn points out, strategies of deviance and accommodation have differing personal costs.

Career/academic guidance

Rarely did the respondents experience a smooth transfer from 'A' levels to higher education. A friend or teacher who for some reason (like Nick) took an interest in their welfare was often the catalyst and guiding arm through the process of application and interview. Parents who had little or no knowledge of the education system did their best to suggest courses and/or a line of employment which they regarded as the most respectable career with some prospects. The systematic career advice which should assist a young person in making an appropriate choice was obviously lacking. Rita recalls the uncertainties and fortuitous events that led her to higher education:

> In terms of what I do, I've never really sat down and systematically mapped out and planned my career. I've always got into things accidentally to a certain extent in so far as I ended up in this post. Prior to that I taught in a FE college, did a PhD etc. I applied to universities to do psychology. I only applied because my husband told me to. I didn't know what I wanted to do! I thought: I don't really like nursing, but what else? Even at that stage, because of role models and expectations, even at that stage I was being steered in that direction. My mother thought nursing would be good. I could become a Sister. She didn't know any better either. The person who's now my husband said, 'Why don't you apply to university?' I'd always expressed an interest in psychology and sociology. I applied and got an unconditional offer without an interview from M University.

Rita and her parents wanted her to pursue a good career. However, career guidance had not provided any sense of direction. The family were thrown back on their knowledge or opinions about what was a 'good job'. Rita's mother's views are not unexpected, as nursing was a very respectable career in the Caribbean. Many women who came to England in the 1950-60s followed a nursing career with the idea of 'going back home' with a good job.

Like Nick, Rita had met someone who knew the system and realised that she had the ability to pursue further study. In a previous quote, Rita had referred to the 'natural progression' of many white students through the education system. Without the interest of this white friend, Rita would not have realised her potential. It appears, from Rita's and Nick's experiences, that 'having the academic ability' was not enough. Black students who did not have access to the knowledge and understanding of the options and workings of the education system could end up settling for occupations which did not stretch their mental capacities.

In some cases the individual black student did have firm ideas about the line of study they wished to pursue. But, again, it still seemed to be a 'benevolent' individual who had to provide the ad hoc assistance lacking in the system. Typical examples were late entries to admissions tutors via informal contacts, or the commitment of a member of family or friend. As an admissions tutor myself I have sufficient evidence to support a hypothesis that, on balance, black students apply to HE courses later than the average white student due to an insufficient understanding of the HE institutional process:

> I was sure about what I wanted to do but my careers teachers said if I wasn't sure which line I wanted to go down I should pick something general in the area that covered lots of different things. It was at the last minute I decided to come to Sheffield, I had university places at B and L universities. It was in the old days — we didn't need to have 3 'A's or 2 'A's. M also offered me an unconditional place. My headmaster had contact there, his old mate was the admission tutor.

Overt prejudice in career advice was seldom identified by these individuals. In most cases the school system had not given them positive encouragement, guided channelling or focused assistance in any systematic way. So they were overtly disappointed with the support offered at this stage of their school career. Some subjects were able to recall advice which appeared to be based on racist stereotyping and an obvious disregard for the young person's demonstrated ability of latent potential.

> I had taken English 'A' level in one year and got an 'A' grade. Yes, I was pleased! This was the end of the second year and I was waiting for the results of my second 'A' level. There was little or no guidance as to what I should do next. Mind you I'd rather that 'they' didn't give any advice. Because the advice that they offered at the end of my 'O' levels was appalling (I had taken 9): at the career interview I was advised to look for shop work or sewing in a factory.

Work Experience

Poor career advice and guidance was a significant feature throughout the educational experience of the subjects. They were not surprised that this floundering accompanied them into their working lives.

In common with the school experience, the interest taken by a sole teacher was matched in the work situation by the assistance of one single employer in the agency or business. However this individual support could not protect the life history subjects from overt and covert racist attacks by other colleagues. Curiously it appears that while, at some level, the subjects identified discrimination and prejudice, they nevertheless-allowed themselves to be patronised. Rita said:

> To my amazement I applied to Boots the chemist not knowing what I wanted to do, not having a clear notion of what I was capable of. At that stage I was into italic writing. I would adore writing using different pens. I remember I wrote to Boots in an italic script asking if there were vacancies for shop assistants. I got a letter asking me to come for an interview and I remember the woman there, Mrs A, who had two years since left university with a pharmacy degree, interviewed me. That woman for some unknown reason took to me and even now when I see her occasionally in town she'll want to see me stop and have a conversation, find out what I'm doing. She interviewed me and commented on the beautiful handwriting and spoke to me generally about things. She said, I think you're too bright to be just a shop assistant, why don't you train to be a chemist dispenser helping to dispense the prescriptions? There is a vacancy there. I said yes. I didn't have a clue what a chemist dispenser was. I was a glorified shop assistant but it was one step up from a shop assistant. I started at Boots. I was the only black employee — this was in 1974 when I left school.

> When I think about it I was a bit of a phenomenon, all the name-calling, not malicious, I suppose. I remember being called 'smiley' by the men. Strange questions I used to be asked with regards to likes and dislikes, diets etc. But the people were very nice, because I was a very young 16 year old I was spoilt to a certain extent.

Rita was uncertain about the direction of her career. A 'chance' interest in italic writing had brought her application form to the eye of those selecting and recruiting for a job in a pharmacy. This interest had created an opening for Rita. Sufficient preparation by school careers staff for employment seeking might have created openings in other areas.

Mrs A's personal interest in Rita's work experience has parallels with Nick's school experience and the progress of other subjects into Higher Education. Being Mrs A's protege did not protect Rita from being viewed as a culturally curious figure. The respondents spoke about their differing levels of consciousness and varied methods of dealing with racially sensitive encounters. Some chose to use humour as a form of resistance. Others refused to be patronised or pathologised and measured the consequences of confrontation and being labelled aggressive. During the conversations the respondents and I discussed the view that aggression could be seen as a 'source and strategy for survival'. Being able to distinguish intentional and unintentional racism was also much discussed.

In certain circumstances, humour was not deemed to be an appropriate response. The subjects considered that it was essential that they registered their dissatisfaction with what they experienced as racist behaviour, whether individual or institutional. Being refused jobs, positions, opportunities they were eligible for, on spurious and inadequate grounds were common experiences. On one occasion Kevin felt that a direct challenge was his only option. Being denied an 'available' opening for his professional development was a critical issue which demanded an assertive challenge.

Being unsupported in these times of challenges can leave an individual feeling bruised and despondent. Finding alliances, and experiencing personal affirmation can help to regenerate flagging spirits for the next encounter. Kevin's experience was painful.

> My personal life at this time in terms of teaching took a knock. I applied to do a Master's Degree. I was accepted by the University and accepted by the education authority. It was almost a foregone conclusion. The current head at the school had OK'd it. In the interim period up to Christmas he'd left. The new head came in. I was waiting to hear from my authority confirmation re my secondment. I heard nothing. November, December, went by. In January, I phoned the Education Department for information. This apologetic guy slightly embarrassed at the other end said, 'Sorry Mr Q I don't know how to say this but between me and you and the gate post we had provided the money for you and it was OK for you to go, but your school couldn't (wouldn't) release you.' No one had the decency to say something to me.
>
> The new head had said he would see every member of staff at the start of term to discuss workload. I remember, when it was the turn for my workload interview I kept getting put off and put off. When I found out about his decision I wanted to see the man but he kept putting me off with all sorts of excuses like fire alarms etc.! Eventually I saw him. He didn't know that I knew. I said I wanted to talk about my secondment. He started to say 'Oh well, you understand that it's very difficult to get

> secondment these days.' I said, 'I know that I got it and I know that the School hasn't given me permission and I'd like to know why.'
>
> I think it was the first time, certainly at that school, that he had been challenged in that way. He started to bluster and blush. He'd just made this arbitrary decision. Whether it was done in terms of 'race' or 'paternalism', in that he liked to be the one to sponsor people, I don't know.
>
> I was mad about it, but because of naivety, lack of political awareness, whatever, I did nothing. It would never happen to me now. But after that I got depressed, despondent — there was the drive, urge to move to go elsewhere to find another experience.

Rarely did the life history subjects recall being consciously assisted to progress in their work experiences via institutional process. Obstructive and cynical colleagues also marred their paths to progress. Those life history subjects who had spent time in the field of teaching agreed that the experiences of black pupils often evoked memories of their own career path. Kevin recalled his experiences:

> Another kid I know, J, now also doing his housing Degree. These people are really coming on now. I remember when I was teaching him in the 4th year. I remember almost being in tears over the guy's frustration, he talked patois at home. That's what he talked with his contemporaries. But at school he's expected to write English or History essays and there were problems. All teachers were doing was correcting his work by saying, 'it shouldn't be was, it should be is' — that kind of stuff. It just denies and fails to recognise the need of English as a foreign language to Creole speakers. All these kind of issues, all these kinds of things inside me. I knew that things were not quite right but 'what was wrong?' and 'what could I do?' I started to get more interested in the 'Black thing' in Sheffield, the educational problem. That's when we started to have a lot of meetings with the careers service. We started a parent support group at H school with the knowledge of the head. He thought 'it was a good thing', but never came to any meetings. It was a 'feather in cap'. We did a lot of work in the community. It was at that time that others who are now involved in race issues got involved and started to make some moves.

Having had similar experiences in his own school career, as a teacher, Kevin felt a need to assist the black children. Offering individual assistance was one method of challenging the system. Kevin found that collective challenge and a focus on key areas of the system were equally effective. On the one hand he counselled, supported and assisted students like J. He also identified areas in the system which could be challenged. With a collective voice, Kevin, like-minded professionals and other community members formed pressure groups which challenged power structures. Such groups acknowledged that in the 'politics of race', various approaches were available as options. As a group they had to decide how best to champion the cause of the black community.

Working in partnership with white colleagues was an obvious option; the headmaster had 'given his approval, he'd even thought it was a good idea'. Kevin indicates his suspicion of the head's motive — 'feather in cap'. There seemed to be little if any tangible support from this colleague: 'he never came to any of the meetings'.Taking the responsibility to challenge eurocentric and racist institutions, with or without the help of white colleagues, is a common option. Being confident about the views and needs of their community, identifying their role and responsibilities in the scenario, led many of these respondents to join pressure groups which aimed to improve services to the community.

Other respondents examined the often ambivalent position of black professionals working in welfare organisations. In the USA the black middle class is said to be sufficiently defined to warrant academic investigations as 'the marginal person', the member of an ethnic group who feels alienated from both the majority and minority community (Brown, 1989). Nick appeared to be aware of this dilemma when he stated:

> I sound like a typical British grammar school-college type but I also know about black culture and am a part of it despite my work.

He suggested that his position is a comfortable 'bi-cultural existence'. However, in England a number of black professionals appear to experience some difficulty in being on the one hand members of the black community and, on the other hand, members of white racist organisations which oppress black people. Liverpool (1986) identifies 'flight' as a defence mechanism employed by black workers who fear over-identification with one group or another. To illustrate this point, Liverpool cites the black social worker who wore formal dress and spoke standard English at work but could be seen after work amongst his black peers dressed as a Rastafarian and speaking patois. By adopting dual identities, one for the organisation and one for the outside, this black worker appeared (to Liverpool) to be showing signs of a split personality.

Nick wanted to establish, with me, his cultural position. For some black individuals, especially black professionals, the accusation of being a 'coconut' or 'white-washed' — black on the outside and white on the inside — is deeply offensive. Black professionals like Nick, who work in the welfare services, can face a further difficulty. Given the size of the black communities in towns like Sheffield, black workers are likely to socialise in the same areas as they work. Black professionals are easily identified and held up as positive role models by the black community. However, the elevated position can be compromised when a black social worker is forced to intervene in cases such as alleged child abuse. In a tightly woven community the black worker can find themselves isolated. Issues of confidentiality can mean that there is no opportunity to explain why a particular action was taken. Owen (1980) offers advice to black workers: they should be prepared for the times when they question their own commitment and responsibility to the black community. He suggests that during these periods of depression and loneliness it is imperative that the black worker be able to confide in a sympathetic listener about job-related problems as well as racial feelings, for the sake of their (the black worker's) mental health.

In the following chapter quotations which focus on issues of religion or the subject's affiliation to certain sects will be discussed.

Chapter 5

Religion-related themes

This chapter collates a range of themes which relate to the subjects' affiliation with religion. As in chapter four, the themes are drawn from quotes lifted directly from the transcripts. The thematic headings are: self-discipline, benefits of church attendance, determination and resilience, disenchantment with religion, owning parental religion. Descriptive interjections are intended to help the reader to gain a fuller picture of the subjects and their situation. Religion is presented by the subjects as an all-pervasive phenomenon which had significant impact on their early lives. The respondents described how during their late adolescence it became evident that a decision-making process was on-going — they chose either to follow family traditions and embrace the religion of their childhood, or to reject aspects of an integral part of their upbringing.

Self-discipline

The subjects spoke at length about various experiences which would have justifiably caused them overt anger. Verbal and physical confrontations, often generated by racial stereotyping or racism by teachers or children, could legitimately have been met with aggression or anger. The respondents shared their views about being able to express anger or distress as honest forms of self-expression. They recognised that such behaviour could be seen as a survival mechanism rather than a pathological response.

The respondents told of their justified and constructive use of anger on certain occasions. There was no doubt that constructive use of anger was preferred to self-criticism, self-harm or other forms of misdirected anger.

Being willing to suppress their justified emotions of anger, frustration and moral indignation despite severe provocation, appeared to be a resource which assisted these life history subjects. They debated the pros and cons of this approach. A number of them linked this capacity with their religious upbringing.

> Actually becoming a Christian has had an effect on my behaviour at school, because at that time I thought.... there were times when kids would give me a lot of stick and they would be name-calling and all these kinds of things, I told them off but I was not going to get involved in any sort of physical...

In Chapter two I outline the ideological position of the Seventh Day Adventist and Pentecostal churches. Both these groups evidenced an appreciation of and commitment to many dominant societal values. Jason refers to the internalisation of these views. Many respondents realised that values of self-respect, respect for adults and for property — all undisputed values in their home settings — held little weight with a number of their peers in school. They were shocked and bewildered at the behaviour and attitudes of their school-mates. Contrary to the destructive and verbally abusive approach of others in their class, a number of the life history subjects aimed to be 'good pupils'. Jason recalls his experiences in secondary school:

> It's almost a Protestant ethic in a way to work hard to do your best at things, to shun badness. That's why when I was talking about some of the things I encountered at HS I was shocked. Wanton vandalism, just doing it for the sake of it, wanton filth and degradation. I just recoil from those things and my religious background has played some kind of part in that.

The respondents found that being able to distinguish between constructive and destructive uses of anger was essential for social interaction. By being aware that adults and peers might be deliberately trying to provoke a particular response, respondents were able to consciously order their behaviour, thus avoiding the negative consequences that come from the social labelling which is attached to being 'angry or out of control'.

> I suppose there are fewer confrontations in a way because you are already disciplining yourself. You're one step ahead of other people, of what's going on. Where previously you would have been annoyed to the point of physical violence, you can tell people off, make sure that they know what you think and feel without using the same tactics as them.

Teachers might not readily accept a view of their professional task that identifies the need for control and containing children as a higher priority than the wish to provide a nurturing environment in which children can develop. However, in Britain the political and socio-economic climate has had a severe impact on the teaching profession. Many teachers feel disillusioned, while many others are leaving the profession due to stress-related complaints or low wages (Goodson, 1992).

There are many reasons why interpersonal relationships between teachers and pupils are suffering in the current climate. Due to regular changes in government regulations, teacher workloads are constantly increasing, with the result that teachers do not have sufficient time to befriend or take as much personal interest in their pupils as they would wish. Consequently the quieter pupils who appear to be functioning within the required parameters without demanding too much additional assistance or pastoral care, may be regarded as 'good pupils'. Becker (1952) explores these notions of the 'ideal pupil'.

In her secondary school Joan met a great deal of what she experienced as racial prejudice, in a variety of forms. She felt personally wounded by these experiences. From the following quote, and other sections of her conversation, one suspects that she would have appreciated time and space to discuss these experiences. At the time she felt that there was little point in going to the teachers, as she was sure that they would not understand her perceptions and emotions. Instead she felt that on balance it was better to discuss her problems elsewhere, while continuing to project the image of a 'good pupil'.

> I found that a lot of teachers were sympathetic to me, they didn't really understand what was going on inside me. They thought: she behaves well, she's quiet. They were all very nice, I mean uniformly nice to me.

Religious observance and Church attendance

Religious observance and church attendance were two areas that permeated the conversations. Respondents viewed their lives as inevitably and indelibly influenced by church membership. The influences of formative years are further discussed elsewhere. In a number of the following quotes the subjects discuss the variety and extent of this influence. Individual and community benefits are identified as a central part of church attendance and religious observance.

Religion played a significant role in the lives of all the life history subjects. Church attendance was just one aspect of their experience. Being a 'church member' influenced their lives in a profound and all-encompassing way. In general, the subjects viewed their church membership as having a positive impact on their lives. Kevin reflects on experiences in his home when he was an adolescent:

> If there was a religious film on it wouldn't matter what was on the other side, football or anything. I must have seen 'The Robe' twelve times. Even if they weren't Bible bashing, the Christian religion had an influence in the home. We knew our Bible well. It was pervasive, it filtered through. It was effective. I wasn't compelled, it just filtered through. I was brought up in an environment or climate of the church.

In Kevin's home there appeared to be undisputed respect for religious things. The sacred was elevated above the secular in all aspects of domestic routines. On reflection, Kevin wondered why family members needed what seemed to be a constant reminder of their beliefs. He felt that it was important for family members to see their religious beliefs presented on what is often a purely secular medium. The film 'The Robe' is a biographical account of the life and death of Christ. A seasonal showing of this film (maybe Easter), was regarded in Kevin's house as an opportunity to engage in worship of a different dimension, whereas other Christians might reject the commercial, materialistic edge to such 'seasonal Christianity'. Indeed others might regard the merging of secular medium and sacred subject matter as inappropriate.

In this last quote Kevin hints at a possible difference of opinion between family members on the extent to which religious matters merited such priority. Could it be that Kevin harboured some resentment at having to watch this film so often? Might he have preferred to watch a football match or some other programme? Even if his parents needed a constant reminder of the availability of 'a shield against a meaningless society', Kevin seemed less keen. As an adolescent he was developing an individualised view of God, even though he was generally active in Church. He had an interest in religion but was not overly concerned with religious issues. Kevin was demonstrating a reluctance to follow parental views on religion.

Kevin draws a picture of a home environment where religion was a covert, subtle part of his primary socialisation. He had been involved with it for so long that it was a regular, systematic part of family values and family routine. He did not need to be compelled.

Others had what appears to be a much more overt, evangelical religious upbringing. Jason recalls his own experience:

> I had a very strict upbringing, you couldn't play cricket on Sunday. You had to read the Bible and go to church. We learnt quite a lot from it.

Jason's religious upbringing might be regarded as tantamount to religious indoctrination. It appears that Jason would have preferred to play cricket! From the quote it does not seem that Jason would have volunteered to read his Bible. However, as with other aspects of family values, Jason and other respondents took the opportunity during conversations to register respect and gratitude for their parents' opinions and demands.

Many of the respondents reflected on the benefits of being a church member. Social and psychological benefits appeared to be central to their experience. Conscious external disciplines as well as the sense of belonging, being valued and cared for by humans and the divine were often recalled as family experiences.

Nick has no doubt about the role religion played in his home, for his family and in his own life. In their conversations, Nick and Jason talked about the all-encompassing nature of their church membership. The following quotes have been chosen to highlight and underline specific aspects of church membership which the respondents deemed to be beneficial. Andrew recalled his 'Bible study' periods as a child:

> I think it helps you to read because you have learnt various passages and recited these at Sunday school in the morning. All very good

> training in one's life. I think also to do things and to do it well and to be appreciated for it does help you to go on and do other things.

Being appreciated in the church setting gave respondents a sense of reassurance and self-validation. Jackie experienced a typical welcome when she visited a new church. She describes the event:

> At church everyone is responsible for you. I went along there; in fact there were quite a number of black people there. The first person I met was from Jamaica. I said 'I've just come, where shall I sit?'. He immediately took me and put me to sit next to his wife and he looked after me ever since. They introduced me to others. They took me under their wing.

Calley (1965) pointed out the extent to which church members cared for each other. In the earlier, immigration days they would care for each other's children and lend each other money. They also shared their social and recreational activities with one another. The caring attitude, youth and adult, pervaded the membership. This environment gave the reinforcement they needed to deal with regular emotion and psychological 'onslaught'. Many of the respondents' parents viewed their life away from the church as potentially isolating. Jackie outlines some of the activities the church provides for youth:

> We would go to church a couple of evenings a week. Convention was in the summer and was a major event. We would go on Sunday school day trips — that was the only time we got to see the seaside. I was with a lot of my peer group friends. School and church were the two places I spent most of my time.

Church membership helped to provide a personal and social identity for many of the subjects, their family members and peers.

Determination and Resilience

During conversations the subjects identified the hurdles that society had erected and the processes they had to go through in order to achieve their educational aspirations. These issues gave them a great deal to reflect upon. In attempting to understand what sustained them through very difficult times, most of them scanned their complete life history, examining various events and the role played by various individuals.

I now quote at length from the transcripts of Nick's life history to present a more complete picture of his experiences. These quotes locate some examples of where he demonstrated aspects of his determination and resilience in relation to acquiring his education.

> When I was taking 'O' levels I would say I loved learning and I couldn't understand why other kids did not love learning as I did. And then you go through a process which knocks, dents, bruises — becoming de-skilled. Disillusion was all around me. I remember being able to read and avidly wanting to read. And wanting to know and wanting to learn books off by heart. There's still an element of that love of learning. And people still have it. It's a process you have to go through to learn, learning, research, finding out. A love of academia almost for its sake irrespective of almost what you are studying. There's an element of that in me.
>
> So many different things shape you at different times. When I did the HND Business Studies, I was to all intents and purposes a dropout at that stage. I was doing the least amount that I thought would get me a job in the area I thought I wanted at that time. When I went back to the Poly and did the BA there were elements in that course that reawaken that love for learning. Some of it was rubbish, but that spark is still there. At the moment I'm very tired and the thought of studying, well I think I'd like to do it, but....
>
> I don't think I consciously equated good education with a good job in that way. I think it's got something to do with feelings about status and self-worth. Having education seems to have something to do with feelings about status and self-worth. Having education seems to be one of the ways I feel worthwhile. Maybe worthwhile is not the right word, but a sense of achievement having done something, struggled for something. And a little element of proving people wrong or right. Like the guy who was in charge of the sales section at the steel firm, who went on about teaching being hard. He said 'have you thought about this and that'! It was like two fingers to him subconsciously. Also parents, proving other people right. Strange, I've never thought about that before but it's true — the fact that I got on and their struggles were not in vain. What they believe came through in the end and there were other people who thought you've got something. It's

> also about being black. You've always got something to prove to yourself. You can't just go through the system. It's not correct to think you've got to do something to prove that you are OK or worthy. Our position in this society means that you can't 'drift with the tide', because you don't belong in the tide. Sometimes you have to justify your existence, if not economically maybe educationally.

Nick described himself as having an innate love for learning. If this love had been fostered and nurtured, he believed, he would have pursued postgraduate studies at an early stage. He is resentful of the unnecessary hurdles which education establishments and employers required him to scale. The process of being knocked, dented and de-skilled refers to events at school, college and polytechnic when his confidence was severely shaken. Unsympathetic, hostile and unsupportive teachers were part of his early school experiences. During college he faced an overtly eurocentric and covertly racist curriculum which left him suspicious of the role and function of education. While reflecting on his varied experiences of education Nick was aware of the option to 'drop out' and reject education. Given his sociological understanding of the role and status of education this could have been a real choice. He had obviously considered 'mediocracy' as a strategy for getting through the education system. He said 'I was doing the least amount that I thought would get me a job in the area I thought I wanted at the time'.

There is much evidence in the research literature to suggest that many young black people reject British education and they regard it as a politically biased process which socialises particular groups for particular roles in society. Nick's determination to succeed educationally was driven by that view of himself as a young black person in Britain.

For him there was a subconscious motivating force which, despite setbacks, enabled him to pursue his aspirations. Economic success in terms of wealth did not appear to be a feasible option. However, by achieving academic qualifications which might open the doors of economic and employment opportunity, he might sustain a sense of self-worth.

We can see that Nick felt the need to succeed because of his own personal motivation but also in response to the views and expectations of others. The negative expectations or lack of support from white teachers was probably based on their stereotypical racist assumptions about him as an African-Caribbean male. Mac and Ghaill (1988) highlights the mode of intervention which results from teachers' stereotypical view of African-Caribbean pupils and describes the teachers' common sense perceptions of 'rebellious' African-Caribbean pupils, and the visible forms of resistance used by the pupils to challenge these stereotypes.

Nick had encountered these stereotypical views and attitudes at school and at work. The employer at the steel firm obviously felt that teaching, as a profession, was beyond Nick's abilities. Nick saw his academic achievement as a belated but significant response. Having a professional position from which he could positively contribute gave him a sense of pride which he knew would be shared by his parents. And through the reflexive process of conversation he recalled the consistent support, personal interest and self-confidence that came from his parents' belief in his abilities.

Nick has also outlined a range of influences that were present in his life and had some impact on his academic aspirations. He refers to the role of his subconscious motivation in his quest for academic success.

Angela, too, reflected on this aspect in her life history conversation. She said:

> I wouldn't say that consciously religion has played a significant part in influencing my aspirations or asserting my determination. I wouldn't say consciously, but there must have been a driving force. I haven't turned my back on religion. I used to pray a lot... I do, when things become unbearable.

For Angela there was at the subconscious level an underlying driving force that enabled her to struggle against opposition. She regarded her religious upbringing and affiliations as a subconscious but significant factor in the undercurrent of her motivation.

She identifies the role played by religion in her life. She regards it as a 'driving force' which enabled her to deal with oppression. By offering her self-affirmation, religion empowered her. Like Nick, she was aware of the negative views and expectations of her held by society. It would have been possible for her and many other respondents to succumb to the negative messages. They could have internalise society's negative opinions and thus created a personal disability.

Jackie seemed to be aware of this dilemma when she said:

> Unless you get to the point where you stop being rebellious and hateful and start to be rational you are going to be destroyed by the whole thing. You are going to be so involved in counteracting the racism that you encounter in a negative way that you are going to destroy yourself with hatred. You are going to destroy your chances of getting anywhere in school.

Many individuals in the African-Caribbean community experience a sense of resentment and hostility at society's systematic oppression. The personal investments of energy used to sustain this justifiable anger could be self-destructive. Jackie realised that by conserving her creative energies she could invest in her academic pursuits. She implies that there are positive ways of dealing with racism. Gillborn's (1990) subjects chose their responses to racism from a range of possible options. Those who refused to react to triggers of provocation, who gave some thought to the long-term consequence of their responses, appeared to be those who succeeded in school. Believing that God is in control of all aspects of your life and knowing that he is able to protect you from the pitfalls of racism may enable an individual to feel secure about plans for the future.

Jason felt secure about his future but at times he questioned God about temporary difficulties. He said:

> It makes you see that there can always be positive outworkings. Sometimes I have real problems and I can talk to God about it. I say what is going on, why have you put me here, why have I got to be confronting all this?

Many of the currently religious respondents discussed the positive role of suffering or difficulties in a Christian life. Some regarded problematic situations as essentially learning opportunities through which God could teach them spiritual lessons. Relying on God, humility, patience and needing to reorder priorities were some of the 'lessons' identified by the subjects.

Believing in God and being a Christian gave them a sense of purpose and a sense of direction. They reported the capacity to cope with negative and oppressive experiences. Jason was confident about the role Christianity had played in his life:

> One of the things which being Christian has meant for me is that I've started to work in finding the positive things about myself. That was the real turnaround. It takes quite a few years to be able to overcome a lot of the negatives which have been reinforced by society and everything like school. To get to the point where you can say: I don't care what the people say because I know who I am and what I am and where I am coming from and where I am going. Some people might say that religion is a crutch but as far as I am concerned it has helped me where other people have failed. It has helped me to know the worth of myself despite the efforts of almost all society.

Janet echoed very similar views when she said:

> So I think it's a case of getting to know who you are and being able to convince yourself that even if other people reject you, you still have a sense of identity and I think even more towards the 'O' level stage that began to happen a lot more... I was baptised when I was about 16. I think that had a great effect on my academic work. It gave me even more motivation to do well, for another reason.

The need to please God by 'doing well' is a fundamental aspect of many Christian faiths (see Chapter 2). God's rules and laws could be viewed as punitive. However, many of the respondents stressed their view of God as loving and caring, who rewards good action and provides hope and comfort when in distress. Few respondents, religious or non-religious, emphasised a view of a God primarily to be feared because of his power and authority.

All the respondents spoke of religion as a source of strength in their quest for academic success. Some of the respondents used this source consciously and as a matter of routine, while others had only recently considered the undercurrent of resilience provided by their belief in God.

Kevin said:

> No, I couldn't say I'd turn round and say God help me and sustain me through that, but I think it helps in the resilience that I display. A kind of inner hardness that says there are trials and tribulations but you must keep hammering at them. In that kind of abstract covert way, yes it helped.

Disenchantment with religion

During adolescence and early adulthood the respondents came to differing conclusions about their religious upbringing. Some chose to rebel against parental values and institutional aspects of religion, while others found a personal relationship with what had been their parents' religion. The latter group will be discussed later in this chapter.

Angela expressed the views of many currently non-religious respondents when she said:

> The questioning came round about that age when you question certain things. It's not being able to understand or comprehend everything. Prior to then you take on board the Christian principles. You take things for granted. I haven't since then given it as much thought as I should have done. I do on occasions, when I sense some despair or desperation, I say 'oh God what can I do?' I mean that in a sincere way, not just as something to say.

Having decided not to attend church services, Angela appears to have given little thought to what she had rejected. She seems to have divorce the need to be part of a religious group adhering to the tenets of institutionalised religion from her personal need to communicate with God. The life history conversation gave her the opportunity to reassess the role of God in her life. For Angela, religion was in some ways functional. She could call on God to provide hope and comfort when she was in distress.

Other respondents had given much thought to their reasons for leaving the church. The socio-political role of religious organisations was cited as a fundamental area of concern. Kevin explained:

> I started to question a lot of things in the area of religion. Not necessarily black churches, but... I noted the way the Catholic church and others had been fundamental in spreading colonialism and slavery. I questioned strongly the role of western religions, the conquistadors in Spain who were responsible for butchering many people. Their justification for doing so was converting the heathens. One of the biggest influences on me and a lot of my friends was Alex Haley's 'Roots'. After it a lot of my friends became interested in black politics and black awareness. Those bits about giving them 'Christian names', Kunti Kinti needing to have a Christian name. Tearing from

> them their traditional values and beliefs. You can see why black people are angry at western religions.

When discussing these issues Kevin became animated and passionate. His awareness of the imposition of religion on a range of cultures and peoples over time had left him with a view of a God who did not care for black people. He was prepared to concede that it was religious institutions rather than God that were using the cloak of religion to commit and encourage injustices. However he and other subjects found it difficult to comprehend God's reluctance to intervene on behalf of the oppressed. Andrew unpicks this dilemma by articulating some of the questions. He said:

> I find some of these issues difficult to resolve in my mind. Why the Queen's the head of the Church of England? Why does Mrs Thatcher goes to church? It could be another Prime Minister but she epitomises the contradiction. People fight in the name of God. I just get this feeling, if there is this God, he doesn't do much for black people or the poor. How could we have a royal family with all that wealth and splendour being part of a country where there is such poverty? How could God allow or stand by and allow black people to suffer in the way in which they suffer?

These quotations are further discussed in Chapter 6. Here we note the sense of the growing social and political awareness of the subjects. They are no longer prepared to accept their parents' assessment of historical and current issues. Many of the respondents stated how they felt torn between the functional and the dysfunctional aspects of religion. They valued the self-affirmation and sense of personal strength that came from their religious affiliation and observance. However, the suffering of oppressed groups in England and throughout the world caused them to question the power or compassion of the God they served. This questioning came to a head when they became aware of the suffering of black people.

Kevin became politically aware during his adolescence. Ironically, the oppression of black people in this country was not the main concern for him. He had been introduced to the international political scene and was incensed by what he heard. The growth of militant and radical resistance to white supremacy in America caught his attention. Particular groups and individuals who advocated armed struggle to obtain civil rights were well publicised in America and here in Britain. Kevin recalls:

> Round about the time I took my 'O' levels I became very political because the civil rights movement in America was at its height. The Black Panther organisation started making headlines in this country. I read about George Jackson, about his autobiography. That had a really profound influence on me. I started following what was happening to Angela Davis...

He had found a sense of purpose and community in the religious adherence and observance that had been a central part of his early years. Now, in his adolescent search for his own identity and for meaning in his life, Kevin became disenchanted with the church's response to world oppression.

Joan articulates the tensions and emotional struggles that affected a number of the respondents:

> When I read what was going on in the States and in South Africa it had a profound effect on me. It influenced the way I behaved and my feelings. Now my politics are very clear but then it was feelings. Feelings were coming out which were difficult to articulate, except that you knew that the suffering of black people was wrong. The political struggles of people were affecting me.

Having become aware of the political scene, Joan silently agonised about the blatant injustices that were affecting black people. She yearned for a forum in the black community where it was possible to discuss these issues. Family members seemed unwilling to enter into the debate. Church members implied that God knew best and that because he was in charge all would be well. This tendency to pacify left Joan feeling that issues of social concern were of no real significance to her church brethren. Elsewhere I discuss the black religious community's response to this accusation of social irresponsibility.

The searching and questioning, idealism and militancy converged in Joan's mind. She resolved the situation by leaving the church and overtly pursuing her political concerns about black people's oppression.

Owning their parents' religion

As children, many of the respondents were taken to church with their parents or other members of the family. As they grew up they had to decide whether to reject or accept these religious beliefs as relevant to their own lives. One thing they often considered was the potential contempt and ridicule a religious lifestyle might provoke in their more secular-minded peers.

In his late adolescence and early adult years Jason had already made a personal decision about how to develop a special closeness with God. His relationship with God became more serious and personalised. He described his systematic bible study routine as follows:

> On the religious side, things took on a different meaning as I grew older. It started to be something I got involved in because I wanted to do it, not because my parents made me go to church. I mean I used to take my bible to college everyday to read. I always used to make a point of spending some time from one o'clock each day. I'd set aside about 10 mins and I would read something. You know it was something I was doing at 17 or 18. I didn't sit down in the coffee lounge! That was never conducive. I use to take myself off at lunch time and find a little space.

Jason's college timetable left him with some spare time. Most of the students spend these 'free periods' and break-times together. The college provided a range of activities; a large recreation room boasted a few pool tables, a few table tennis tables and other games. Jason was an athletic young man, good at many different sports. He was able to play table tennis to a high standard. Taking himself off each day at 1.00 pm, the middle of the lunch break, was not an easy decision. He had to justify this 'hermit-like' behaviour to his friends. Explaining to them that his personal study time was a voluntary activity was not easy. His college friends on the whole were not Christians, and they struggled to understand his personal need for this activity. Some of his friends thought that a dispensation, or permission from his minister would allow him more freedom.

Following his parents' religion during childhood had been a taken-for-granted exercise. He attended church every week. His friends attended the same church. He was involved in many of the activities. Indeed he and his family were part of the fabric of the church; they saw the church as a central feature in their lives. As he grew older Jason felt a need to discover and develop a more personal relationship with a more personalised God. Church activities and communal worship twice a week were important to him, but he also needed the personal study time to explore and establish his understanding of God.

Because they live in a predominantly secular society the respondents were conscious of the tendency for the criticisms of their peers to impact on their own beliefs. So they articulated the reasons they valued their religions and critically examined their views of non-believers. Mary said:

> Our religion is very strict. We don't wear jewellery, make up, don't go to discos and we don't drink alcohol. People think life is really difficult and we are cut off. If it was difficult, you wouldn't be in there if it was a constant struggle. You need to be happy in what you are doing. Others think it's a problem not drinking or smoking. I must talk about my religion a lot. They say so at work. I'm glad because it shows I am not ashamed of what I am doing. When white people look at it and analyse it they think 'oh they are just uneducated black people'. So many of us are educated. They're talking rubbish. It isn't like Calvinism and other thinkers who say, you work hard here and get your reward in heaven. 'Pie in the sky.' We also get rewards here. There was a school of thought that said if you worship God and get baptised there's no need to be ambitious career-wise. But we think if God's given you a brain you should use it. Then you can contribute. Put something back into church, help others, the people, the nation. To progress, the church needs teachers in the church to teach spiritually but also to teach about the outside world.

Mary is an active member of the church. Because it is so important to her she finds herself discussing her beliefs with her work colleagues. From these encounters and other discussion and comments from non-Christians, Mary has come to understand their negative even offensive views about black Christianity. Although they may feel reluctant to articulate these views, white non-Christians often regard black sects as a group of uneducated, superstitious black people. Their worship sessions are regarded as primitive, musically vibrant but lacking the intellectual content that is fundamental to white Christianity.

In this quote Mary reflects on the standards and boundaries offered by her Church. She describes them as 'strict' and then goes on to explain that she finds her religious life enjoyable. She does not see a contradiction in her views, rather she gives value to the religious principles that form an integral part of her life style. Mary is clear that her religion offers her security in life after death. However, that futuristic offer is not the sole or most significant aspect of her church involvement. She outlines how the Church's view of individual responsibility leads the members to be contributing citizens rather than pathetic victims. Mary has come to these conclusions through her personal investment in examining and exploring what religious attendance and adherence has meant for her. Older family members had taken Mary to church since she was a child but now her participation and involvement was self-motivated. She had decided that she valued a religious life style.

The respondents saw their religious upbringing as central to and providing guiding principles for the daily interaction with peers in work settings. Colleagues were often curious to know about the philosophies and beliefs held by the respondents. Admiration and ridicule were two contrasting yet common responses from friends and work colleagues.

Russell described his interaction with work colleagues and their view of him.

> I found that at work, especially when I went at PP, it was a new experience. At home you were brought up to respect people older than yourself. You were also taught to treat women as ladies. And then to go to somewhere like PP factory. You get the roughest of the rough. I don't know, I think it was a shock to the system. The way I heard women swearing. The way the young lads talked to the older men. I don't know, I suppose I stood out because I was very particular in the way that I talked to people. You're working together you should show them respect. I was brought up that way. I heard some of the young guys swearing at the older guys. Many of them wanted to know abut the Sabbath issues, and why I finished early on Friday. They wanted to get to know your beliefs. Although they ridiculed you, they were still looking at you and watching you. Any time you make a move in the wrong direction they were quick to pull you up, although initially it looks as if they are not really bothered about what you are talking about.

Russell continues:

> I'll never forget — once I was helping one of the older guys lift something off a machine. But he hadn't got hold of it properly. We were lifting it and all of a sudden it came down and it dropped on my finger. It hurt me like I don't know what! All I did was 'Ssssss'. I put my hand under my arm and went about saying 'Ssssss'. The others in the workshop were all watching me. I wasn't really paying any attention at the time. When I settled down they looked at my finger and said 'Oh, you have to go and get that seen to'. When I came back they said to me, 'You didn't swear! We were waiting for them words to come flying out ten to the dozen'. They added 'What did you do, bite your tongue?' I said: It never entered my mind. Nothing like that ever entered my mind. If something had dropped on my finger it's 'Sssssss' — that was the first reaction, to put it under my arm and try to comfort the pain, you know? They may think that it's a pretence, this religion business.... But when something spontaneous like that happens, it will show the real you. It will show.

Reflecting on that and other experiences Russell said:

> I think in a way they respected me for what I was. For what I believe in.... Because I remember that sometimes at coffee break times we used to have discussions. There were other guys there that said they went to church. They didn't go every week. They are always smoking and complaining. I always remembered one of the older guys. He said, I don't mind people who say they are religious and stick by it. Like, I mean, I respect Russell because whatever he says, he is doing. But you and Johnny, you say one thing and you do another. So obviously I could see from those comments that I was making an impression. They do watch you and although they might not be paying any attention, they listen to what you say and see whether you're saying what you're doing.

Russell found the crude macho environment of the factory floor a unwelcoming place to practice his religion. It was obvious that his workmates did not share his opinions or values. However he felt that it was necessary to share his beliefs by explaining his religion to his colleagues. Equally, he felt that by behaving in a respectful manner he would be demonstrating the principles that underpinned his religious beliefs. His behaviour earned him a good reputation. Comparisons were made between Russell's practice of his beliefs and other work colleagues with similar religious beliefs.

With hindsight, Russell describes the loneliness of his experience. He often felt an overwhelming sense of isolation. He was respected in the factory and the fact that he was not a discredit to his fellow Christians was reassuring to him, but being under constant surveillance, being observed and watched for the slightest slip, was an uncomfortable experience.

I am not sure how many of the respondents would have had as much self-control as Russell. The ability to restrain onesself on such an occasion from resorting to bad language, swear words or taking God's name in vain comes after much practice. Controlling his emotions and language had become second nature to Russell. It might have been easier for him if he worked in an environment where his Christian principles were supported rather than challenged or scrutinised.

The respondents who developed a close individual relationship with God spoke about events where it was clear to them that he was working in their lives and for them. Disappointments, frustrated opportunities and rebuffs were all regarded as God's way of intervening in their lives. As a prelude to describing the events at college, Russell said:

> You begin to see now where it is you and Christ working together. You see the way that God can help and work in your life. I think you notice things like asking for a job or getting the job. You start to put your trust in the Lord and you believe that the Lord makes openings and opportunities.

He then spoke at length about difficulties he faced while at the polytechnic. Science and mathematical subjects appeared to be the most problematic for the respondents who were denied adequate tuition at junior and secondary school level. At times, Russell felt that he was struggling without human or divine assistance. He came to see that his disappointments were never unbearably crushing episodes which were permanent. Rather he has subsequently seen how God had led him through disappointments, as learning experiences which he now regards as positive and purposeful.

> I often think about the struggles I had in getting my degree. I think it was the best way for me to have come, because at school Christ didn't

> have any part in my life. The way I succeeded, certain situations that I went through, I was coming to know God better. I was learning to trust in God more. If I had gone the easier way, I might have left God out. I came to know God and saw how he helped me. I can see the relevance of having Christ in my life.

Russell described one occasion during his degree studies. He told me how God clearly demonstrated his interest in human affairs and his ability and capacity to help. Russell said:

> I always remember one Sunday while I was studying for my degree. I said, Lord I can't understand why you brought me here to struggle like this. You know you told me to try and told me to progress. I'm here struggling; you know, I'm struggling to keep up with the work. There's no way I seem to be able to cope with the work load they are putting on me. I come home working. Working all the time. I work at weekends. I come home do more work. I still can't get on top of any of the work.
>
> Anyway I said this prayer. Low and behold the next day I went to the college. We were doing a laboratory experiment and as we finished it one of the black guys there, a technician, just came up to me and said: if you've got any problems, you know, just come and look for me. I'm down here most times you know, I'll help you with whatever I can. I thought 'that was an answer to prayer'. I mean, I'd never seen him before. Never said anything to him. He was actually looking after the laboratory and he just came and approached me like that. So I thought, this is an offer I can't refuse. He helped me a lot, coaching me through a lot of the work. He gave me the extra help that I needed. I knew that it was God that sent assistance.

This experience with prayer was just one that happened to Russell. Other respondents reported a number of 'answered prayers' in relation to their studies.

For members of many black sects, prayer is a genuine form of communication with God. The reciting of prepared prayers are rarely part of public or private worship. In prayer, respondents believed that they could speak with God, asking him for whatever they need. Remembering to thank God for his previous blessings is an important dimension to prayer.

Russell's prayer does not highlight this aspect but he would endorse the words of Philippians 4:6:

> Be careful for nothing; but in everything by prayer and supplication with thanksgiving let your requests be made known unto God.

The respondents who currently attend church services agreed that prayers were a central feature of their public worship as well as their private spiritual devotion. Russell believed that prayer is the key in the hand of faith to unlock heaven's storehouse, where are treasured the boundless resources of Omnipotence (White, 1971). Beyond that, he felt that he would be undermining the power of God by refusing to ask for and rely on God's power. He points to this poem by Archbishop Trench as a summary of his view:

> Lord what a change within us one short hour
> Spent in Thy presence will prevail to make!
> What heavy burdens from our bosom take!
> What parched grounds refresh, as with a shower!
> We kneel, and all around us seems to lower!
> We rise, and all, the distant and the near
> Stands forth in sunny outline, brave and clear.
> We kneel, how weak. We rise, how full of power!
> Why, therefore should we do ourselves this wrong?
> Or others, that we are not always strong.
> That we are ever overborne with care,
> That we should ever weak or heartless be,
> Anxious or troubled, when with us in prayer
> And joy and strength and courage are with Thee?

An immediate, direct answer for Russell was the result of his prayer or that occasion. However, the respondents talked about other situations when they had to wait for an answer to prayer. The wait did not dishearten them if they continued to believe that God loved and cared for them and would at the right time grant their requests. Religion was for these respondents a personal relationship with a caring God.

The next Chapter considers the respondents' views of religion as a functional and at times dysfunctional phenomenon in their lives.

Chapter 6

Interpretation and analysis of religion-related themes

The previous chapters have presented a number of themes which emerged as pertinent to the life history subjects during the conversations. As anticipated, one of the common themes running through these interviews was the subjects' religious views and the impact of a religious upbringing on their lives. This common theme colours all the data and appears to deserve a significant place in the process of interpretation and analysis. Some consideration has already been given to a number of the other themes in previous British and international research. However, there is a paucity of information on the relationship between black people, religion and education in the British context. I therefore thought it appropriate to focus a whole chapter on the exploration of themes which are strongly or more directly related to the subjects' association with religion and religious organisations.

Interpretive studies need a focus — if not they become unwieldy and cumbersome. My focus in this chapter is the need to interpret and analyse the apparent ways in which religion influences and impacts on the lives of black British people and the extent to which this influence helps to determine their academic success. Analysis here refers to the use of broad theoretical constructs to interpret the experiences of the respondents. In an attempt to balance out the temptation to immerse myself in an 'objective' debate which gives little value to the subject's view, I have tried to ensure that the need to interpret the respondents' experiences is central to this chapter. My use of interpretation in this chapter is intended to build on the respondents' experiences in the previous chapters. Description in itself is not enough. Interpretation must be made and conveyed to the reader, thus making sense of the subjects' accounts of their experiences. It is a process through which the meanings and conceptual structures that organise the subjects' experiences are illuminated, untangled and clarified.

Interpretation is understood to refer to the attempt to explain the meaning of a term, to translate the unfamiliar into the familiar.

> The act of interpreting gives meaning to an experience, the signification, purpose and consequences of a set of experiences for an individual. Once these experiences have been interpreted an understanding of the said experiences can be arrived at. The meaning of an experience can then be comprehended and grasped (Denzin, 1989, p.104).

Denzin suggests that there are two types of interpreters: the people who have actually experienced what has been described and another group, the so-called informed experts, who are often sociologists or anthropologists. He states that these two types of interpreters, 'local' and social scientific, will often give different meanings to the same set of described experiences. Denzin appears to give no consideration to individuals like myself who fit both categories as the 'local social scientist'. However he acknowledges that:

> because interpretation is a temporal process researchers are advised to study those areas of social life where they have some intimate familiarity. By doing so he or she can draw upon the stock of knowledge that has been built up out of previous life experiences (Denzin, p.109).

Drawing on discussions about methodology presented earlier, it is appropriate to remind ourselves that interpretations will falter if they fail to reflect lived experiences. Or if they are highly speculative, making assumptions about the experiences of the individuals without grasping the significance that the respondents themselves give to their experiences.

In trying to understand their own experiences and conduct, individuals have working theories of their own. These theories may be derived from their fellows and/or contained in the oral and printed cultural text of the group. The theories may be based on the 'local knowledge' that individuals and groups have about the experiences that matter to them. These theories 'work' in that they provide meaning to the problematic experiences, and allow persons to deal with the problems that confront them. By exploring these working theories in this chapter I am giving value to the experiences and interpretations outlined by the life history subjects, thus moving towards the major goal of interpretation which is to uncover these theories.

Denzin (1989) usefully pulls together the stages of description, interpretation and understanding:

> Just as description provides the framework for interpretation, so too does interpretation create the conditions for understanding. Understanding is an interactional process. It requires that one person enters into the experience of another and experiences for herself the same or similar experiences experienced by another (p.120).

He views as central the subjective interpretation of another's emotional experience from one's own standpoint. Although Denzin distinguishes between cognitive and emotional understanding, he notes that the two are difficult if not impossible to separate: '... *Shared and sharable emotionally lie at the centre of the process of understanding*' (p.121).

In line with analysis and interpretation as outlined above, I intend to examine in some depth a number of the quoted accounts in previous chapters, unpacking issues raised within them.

This chapter therefore brings together the themes from the last chapter to explore in greater depth the subjects' views on religion and their religious experiences and affiliations. A range of authors will be used as resources for further unpicking the perceptions and experiences of the respondents. A discussion of the definition of 'religious' is an appropriate way to begin. The views of religious and non-religious subjects are then discussed in relation to various events and stages in their lives. The views of the subjects are at times challenged or supported by writers such as Cone (1975) and Miranda (1979).

Many factors influenced my choice of life history subjects. However, given that an aspect of the task was to ascertain the role religion may play in the life of an academic achiever, it seemed valuable to interview both 'religious' and 'non-religious' individuals. 'Religious' is used here to refer to those who are currently regular church attenders and who express some commitment and devotion to all aspects of the religious group's activities. 'Non-religious' refers to those who are not currently attending the services of a church or sect and who express no commitment to participating in the activities of any such group. Before proceeding with the use of the terms religious and non-religious, the working definitions require wider debate which acknowledges other issues.

Definition of 'Religious'

What are the central factors involved in being religious? Are there sufficient similarities between all world religions, such as Christianity, Islam and Buddhism, to permit the term 'religious' to be used wholesale in a meaningful fashion? Several questions seem pertinent: How central is the communal act of worship? Could an individual with a set of beliefs about ultimate reality, who engages in his or her own religious practices not shared by any one else, describe himself or herself as religious? Or could the philosophical defence of and empathy for religious convictions, without a commitment to take a 'stand', be enough to merit the label religious?

Individual, psychological and emotional experiences cannot be ignored or denied. However, in the area of research, much weight has been given to social aspects of religion and far less to the role it plays for the individual psyche, except in time of crisis, death, natural disasters etc (Rowe, 1989). Religion is viewed by such writers as Durkheim, Berger and Marx in various ways — as some form of social delusion, as a device to reinforce the collective identity, as a tool of class exploitation, as an attempt to escape from the world or as an illusion to ease pain or explain the inexplicable. Personal and private experiences can only be deemed as 'religious' by this definition if the experience is linked to the shared orientation of a social group.

Hick (1988) also contributes to the discussion of the term when he asks:

> What do we mean by the term religious? For an enormous range of phenomena have been labelled religious. From the mana-taboo beliefs of primitive peoples to the most exalted forms of ethical theism; from the Brahmanic-Hindu view of the Absolute as a non-personal Unity to the Judaic-Christian and Islamic view of the Abso-

> lute as moral personality; from swarming polytheisms and belief in evil deities who demand the sacrifice of human blood, to the Christian belief in one God, Holy, righteous and loving, creator and ruler of the universe, who seeks kindness and compassion between man and man, and who descends in the self-giving of incarnation to enable men to fulfil his will; and so on through all the wide variety covered by the highly elastic noun 'religion' (pp.136 and 137).

The common factor which Hick can see amidst this complex range is the implicit or explicit belief that humanity's environment is greater than it seems. That interpenetrating the natural, but extending behind and above it, is the supernatural as a larger environment to which human beings must relate themselves through the activities prescribed by their cult.

> The supernatural whether conceived as one or as many, as good or evil, or part good and part evil, as lovable or fearful, to be sought or shunned, figures in some fashion that can be termed religious (p.39).

The extent to which this phenomenon, however defined, influences the lives of individuals is much discussed in the field of social science.

As western societies have become more economically and technologically developed, sociologists have identified a process of secularisation. Such an analysis suggests that the influence of religion in all areas of social life is losing its significance. Religion could currently be seen as a transient, marketable commodity with which one can engage with whatever frequency or intensity one may choose. Wilson (1982) argues that this process of decline is evident in the fall in church attendance, the overall decline in the membership of the Church of England, and the clergy's loss of status. In essence he views the established church as maintaining its institutional presence while lacking a solid base among the general public.

Berger (1976) suggests that religion is not obsolete but is changing its form and therefore a lack of religious observance does not necessarily reflect lack of interest in religious thought. Indeed the theory of subterranean theology (see Martin, 1967) views contemporary religion as going underground, expressing itself more in concern for people and/or beliefs in horoscopes, luck and the supernatural, than an insistence on a gospel. Dalton (1989) highlights the responses of black American churches to the growth in the numbers of AIDS victims in their locality. Rather than condemning the 'sins' of drug-taking, homosexuality, prostitution and stealing — crimes commonly associated with the AIDS virus — the black churches in these areas are giving time and other resources to help affected individuals whatever their religious persuasion. The suggestion that technologically advanced societies deem religion to be an unnecessary aspect of human existence fails to take account of a view of human beings as innately religious. Hick (1988) offers the dichotomy between inclining and determining as an attempt to understand religious behaviour. He views the former as an essential prerequisite which assists in maintaining autonomy in any truly personal relationship between God and humans. In modern western societies individuals are seen to have an innate bias towards this relationship with God. Hick points out the difference from earlier or less developed societies where individuals seemed to have little choice about their religious behaviour and where individual choice was subsumed under a form of social determination. He states that in primitive societies the individual is so entirely moulded by the collective mind of which he is a part, that speculation and doubt are rare occurrences. Any kind of critical thinking on the part of the individual about the common dogmas, the established deities, has been a comparatively late development.

> It is at a comparatively recent stage of development that our cognitive freedom in relation to the divine has become operative. Prior to that, mankind's innate bias towards religion, although not irresistible, was not (as far as we know) in fact resisted, but held an unquestioned sway over men's minds (p.139).

With this debate in mind, I intend to work with the proposed definition of religion which focuses on 'attendance' and 'participation'. The notion of internalisation of belief does not figure strongly in this working definition. Although an important factor, the scope of this research is unable to unpick such a controversial area satisfactorily; it would demand considerable quantitative and qualitative investigation. Elements of religious behaviour such as 'participation' and 'attendance' are generally accepted as differentiating churches from sects (Randall, 1986, p.103). The participatory aspect is a central theme in this study. The wider discussion above, which explores religious and non-religious behaviour, should provide an interpretive framework on which our analysis of black sects can hang. The study of an individual's or a group of individuals' relationship to their church may enable the reader to see various aspects of the life of a sectarian. Locating individuals from particular sects did not present the researcher with significant difficulties.

Locating religious and non-religious subjects

Milroy's' (1980) social network theory provides a valuable structure for making decisions regarding the study's choice of population. I sought to identify two groups, religious persons and non-religious. Locating the 'religious' group was ostensibly an unambiguous task as members of the wider community simply identified church attenders. Similarly, the non-religious group were deemed to be non-attenders and therefore known to friends and other members of the community as non-religious. However, although clearly identified by the community as non-religious, each of these individuals revealed during the life history conversations that they had received regular and in some cases strict religious upbringings as children.

Had my use of Milroy's approach failed to locate the correct cluster? The participants who referred the fieldworker to these apparently 'non-religious' individuals knew them to some extent. However, it seems that this aspect of their lives was unknown, difficult to measure or seemingly so far in their past that it was not significant public knowledge. Despite the insignificance of this dimension to their associates, it is note-worthy that each 'non-religious' participant had a strong and lasting religious history. In terms of the working definition of religion which hangs on the central pegs of attendance and participation, these individuals could not be defined as religious. But the possibility of the lasting effects of early training appears to be an important dimension. Although not currently attenders at any church service nor seeing the need to affiliate themselves to a religious body, these individuals reflected on the positive role religion played during their formative years, their period of primary socialisation and its lasting impact on many facets of their lives.

Throughout the interviews I tried to explore how these participants currently viewed their earlier religious experiences and the influences of them on their adult lives.

> All the kids were brought up in that religion, it played an important role without a doubt.

> Yes my mother was an evangelist at the Pentecostal church so we went to church quite religiously!

The above quotes were typical of the life history subjects' comments on religion in their childhood. They were children in families where religion was important. However, we need to assess the assumption that this aspect of their upbringing would have a lasting impact on their lives. Throughout the history of western thinking the allegedly crucial importance of the pre-school years is substantially documented. Much of the past and present discussion on its significance has focused on the effects of maternal deprivation and the latent consequences of institutionalised child care. Central to the debate is the function of continuity and repetition. Mills (1816) notes that the earliest repetitions of one sensation after another produces the deepest habit. The size and duration of the effects is said to depend largely on factors such as the age of the learner, the potency of the experience, and the amount, intensity and duration of subsequent reinforcement or repetition. From the respondents it was clear that 'reinforcement ' of the religious habit, as defined by Mills, would have left a deep, almost inevitably permanent effect. Quintilian and Fived each underscore the point;

> We are by nature most tenacious of what we have imbibed in our infant years, as the flower, with which you scent vessels when new remains in them (Quintilian c. A.D. 35-100).

> We may convince ourselves through psychological observations on others, that the very impressions which we have forgotten have nevertheless left the deepest trace in our psychic life, and acted as determinants for our whole future development. (Fived, 1910).

That early childhood experiences leave irrevocable or indelible impressions on our lives is a popular notion. However, it is counteracted by an understanding that children are not passive receptors of stimulation but dynamic beings within their environment. The link, therefore, between early childhood experiences and outcomes cannot be regarded as simple.

Subjects' rejection of early childhood values

Despite its positive contribution to their upbringing, these individuals offered many and varied reasons for rejecting what they sometimes referred to as their 'parents' religion'. Although differently framed and presented, the life history subjects' rejection of their childhood religion often stemmed from fundamental concerns about, and disagreement with their churches' socio-political position. Nick said:

> Round about the time I took my 'O' levels I became very political because the civil rights movement in America was at its height and the Black Panther organisation started making headlines in this country. I read about George Jackson, about his autobiography. That had a really profound influence on me. I started following what was happening to Angela Davis.

He continued,

> When I read what was going on in the states and in South Africa it had a profound effect on me. It influenced the way I behaved and my feelings. Now my politics are very clear but then it was feelings, feelings coming out which were difficult to articulate, except that you knew that the suffering of black people was wrong and the political struggles of people were affecting me.

Commonly, the respondents recalled that they were their mid or late teens, and exposed to and engaging with social and political issues through study or a wider friendship network, when they began to question the role of religion. While they struggled with the dilemmas that these issues invoked, they found that the church community lacked the wherewithal and indeed seemed unwilling to create the environment where such issues could be unravelled. As these life history subjects progressed in their academic careers, they were offered avenues for in-depth debate in non-religious circles. They viewed their congregations as possibly unable to examine contradictions and apparent weaknesses in their religious beliefs. When history subjects found that if they raised possibly controversial issues in the area of a discussion and if they drew on social science material to support their argument, Church members were often concerned about the use of non-religious text. Janet said:

> My mother always said to me that I intellectualise church too much and that I thought about it too much. It was all just an act of faith and the more you thought about it the less you would understand. That was the only time she thought that maybe education wasn't such a good thing, she said... I was always asking questions she didn't really like.

Despite the respondents' 'felt' experiences, to accept their assertions without further comment would be to ignore the views held by many members of their sects. Black sectarian groups do not in fact regard non-religious disciplines as necessarily in conflict with religious ideas, philosophies and principles. Absolute rejection and dismissal of non-sanctified — ie biblical and prophetic — ideas is not true of the sects' approach to earthly knowledge. Indeed a Latter-day prophetess for the Seventh-Day Adventist Church, Mrs E White (1971) states that one should:

> procure every advantage within your reach for strengthening the intellect. Let the study of books be combined with useful manual labour.

Many of the respondents felt that they were seeking outlets and channels for wider discussion around areas of moral and social debate. Yet the fine balance between doubt and enquiry appears to be central to the dissatisfaction and dismissal felt by these life history subjects. Had these individuals internalised what some aptly called their 'parents' religion' before they began to question its precepts? Had they indeed been religious or merely attenders and perfunctory participants whose expressed commitments to the principles of the denomination were somewhat shallow? Further exploration of their state of mind just before they finally rejected the religion to which they belonged, reveals that they felt some wider social pressure to resist the negative stereotypical image of the 'irrational primitive religious African'. The need to be accepted as western, rational and white could have led them to question and ultimately reject their socialisation within the sect if not the essence of the religion.

A number of the life history subjects expressed their dissatisfaction with the churches' role in the political, economic and racial oppression of people in many parts of the world, particularly the African and Asian continents and the Caribbean. For many of these individuals the world-wide religious community had failed and is failing to address the need of the underprivileged. Angela said:

> I turned my back on the notion of religion and God and what Jesus Christ was about. I find it difficult to resolve in my mind why the Queen's the head of the Church of England, M. Thatcher goes to church (it could be another prime minister but she epitomises the

> contradiction). There are people fighting in the name of God. I just get this feeling, if there is this God he doesn't do much for black people or the poor. How could we have a royal family with all that wealth and splendour being part of a country where there is so much poverty? How could God allow, or stand by and allow black people to suffer in the way in which they suffer?

Writers such as Miranda (1979) have further analysed this aspect of bible teaching. Miranda (1979), supported by other Christian Marxists, asserts that his studies and his experiences led him to see more and more how the essential meaning of the bible's message has been eluding Christians and their organisation. He views the bible, especially Exodus and the Prophets as the revelation of the transcendent God, the liberator of the oppressed, who fights against the oppressor on their behalf. He suggests that if Christians had not lost sight of this fundamental datum, Christianity down through the ages could not have become such an effective ally of so many structures of economic social and political oppression.

It is unfortunate that Miranda himself falls into the trap of omitting racial oppression. Throughout the bible, New Testament and Old, God and Jesus are portrayed as upholding the link between compassion and justice.

> The violation of the rights of the weak is not condoned, for example Deut. 4:34, 5:15, 7:19, 26:8, Ex 6:6, Ps 136:12, Luke 1:46-47, 53-54 'He put down the mighty from their thrones and raise up the lowly. He filled the hungry with good things and sent the rich away empty.'

Miranda and other writers urge us to rethink the essential meaning of the biblical Christian message as being embraced and enacted by many practicing Christians. His interpretation demonstrates that the response of the life history subjects was not necessarily their only option.

Rejection of religion for its racial oppression

A number of subjects questioned the role of religion in the suffering of black people. Kevin said:

> I started to question a lot of things in that area. Not necessarily the black churches' background. I noted the way the Catholic church and others had been fundamental in spreading colonialism and slavery. I

> questioned strongly the role of western religions and the conquistadors in Spain, who were responsible for butchering many people. Their justification for doing so was converting the heathens. One of the biggest influences on me and a lot of my friends was Alex Haley's 'Roots'. After watching it a lot of my friends became interested in black politics and black awareness. Those bits about giving them 'Christian names', Kunti Kinti needing to have a Christian name. Tearing them from their traditional values, their beliefs. You can see why black people are angry at western religions.

Cone (1975) expands on Miranda's (1979) theme by giving central attention to black oppression. He seeks to provide an analysis of the role of religion in the black person's experience. He notes the theological dialectic which examines God's unwillingness or inability to deliver the oppressed from injustice. God is either presented as a white racist or as a finite being unable to assist in the black person's struggle. Cone concludes that it is the theologian's duty to clarify what the church believes and does about its participation in God's liberating work in the world. As a black theologian, he values highly the affirmation of regular church attendance which enables black people to deal with the dehumanising pressures felt throughout the rest of the week.

> These black people knew that whatever impact white folks had on their lives, with God on their side, white folks could not destroy their humanity(p.39).

However he notes that some black people fail to appreciate this 'facility' in Christianity.

> They have convinced themselves that only the white experience provides the appropriate context for questions and answers concerning things divine (p.39).

The reluctance on the part of the life history candidates to use religious ideology in their adult life reflects a prevailing attitude in African-Caribbean communities. Religion is often seen as the white man's oppressive tool, which continues to chain the minds of black people. Authors such as Cone (1975) and Miranda (1979) have written about the relevance of religious ideology in meeting the social, economic and aesthetic needs of the black community. The range of debate around God's role in the past and present suffering of black people reflects the dialectical process within the African-Caribbean community in Britain. It highlights the dynamics of the evolutionary process which this community is currently undergoing.

Reluctance to attend religious services and engage in all aspects of the religion's activities has caused these non-religious individuals to separate themselves from the close social grouping which was once their extended families. However, all those who no longer regularly attended church services readily admitted to the continued effect of their earlier experiences.

Subjects identify the value of church application

Both the religious and non-religious life history subjects identified areas of their religious upbringing which they rated as beneficial in the advancement of their academic careers. These ranged from the purely instrumental/cognitive areas such as learning to read through frequent bible readings, to the social and emotional support network of the 'church family'. While reflecting on their religious upbringing, a number of the subjects noted that when they were still children they had been introduced to a wide range of conceptual frameworks. They regard these concepts as to some degree extending their intellectual capacity for further study. The philosophical and psychosocial aspects of life, self-confidence, encouragement of the work ethic and self-discipline were all cited as contributing factors to their academic development. Moreover, the religious community provided the black community with a setting where they could relate to others; sharing, consoling and reconciling the many and regular problems of living in a racist society.

The tendency for the black sects and black-led churches, discussed here, to cater for the needs of their congregation is not unique. The Chartists and free churches in 19th century Britain were equally involved with the schooling, housing and other social welfare needs of their congregations. Youth clubs, day centres for the elderly, home helps, and a range of other services which the welfare system is failing to deliver are to some extent being provided by black-led churches. Andrew recalled his early experiences:

> I think it helps you to read because you learn various passages and recite these at Sunday school in the morning. A very good training period in one's life. I think also to do things and to do it well and to be appreciated for it, does help you to go on and do other things.

Sensing a particular responsibility for each church member and particularly, newly converted individuals, was fundamental to the growth of the sects. Neibuhr (1929) underscored the sects' realisation of the need consciously to socialise even the children born into the homes of adult members. Andrew said:

> I can only talk about my own experience, I had a very strict upbringing. I couldn't play cricket on Sunday. You had to read the bible. But we learnt quite a lot from it.

Calley (1965) refers to the genuine affection that exists among members. Love is not only expressed ritually. Members choose one another's company rather than the company of others. They welcome one another to their homes, look after each others' children, help one another to find accommodation and work and sometimes lend or give one another money. Nick recalled:

> It's supplied some kind of framework certainly for our earlier lives. Not just the observance but the religious way of life. The people we knew and mixed with, socialised with, went to church or wherever with, that was important and was the fabric of our life. Our family was within that, our extended family was around that. That was what determined how you did and what you did. Also in there somewhere there was the discipline, the build-up and sustaining of religion. I suppose it was also to do with JA society but I find the two things inextricably bound in some way.

Jackie recalled her first visit to a church:

> I went along there, in fact there were quite a number of black people there. The first person I met was from Jamaica. I said 'I've just come, where shall I sit?' He immediately took me and put me to sit next to his wife and he looked after me ever since. They introduced me to others, they took me under their wing. At church everyone is responsible for you.

Joan recalled the central role church and church members played for her:

> We would go a couple of evenings a week and convention in the summer was a major event, or we would go on Sunday school day trips, that was the only time we got to see the seaside. A lot of them were my peer group friends. School and church were the two places I spent most of my time.

In Chapter one I outlined Gillborn's (1990) research which highlights the confrontational relationship between black children and their teachers as just one aspect of their school experience. The teachers' negative views of black children and their expectations of poor behaviour could become a self-fulfilling prophecy (Rosenberg et al, 1968). In fact, during the 1960s many educationalists argued that black children's failure to succeed in academic pursuits was as a direct result of their internalising of negative stereotypes and pathological views of themselves, which are commonly fostered in British society.

Stone (1981) argues strenuously against the notion which prevailed during the 1960s that black children's academic failure was linked to a poor self concept. She argues that:

> People derive the means to sustain a sense of self from many sources of information about self. Through political, social, literary and musical styles people create alternative sources of self hood. We should not therefore be surprised to find a normal/average distribution of self-concept scores amongst black children living in Britain (p.228).

Stone quotes Abelson's (1977) contribution to the wider debate, insisting that,

> it must be possible for us to regard people as free agents whose actions and avowals are explainable by reasons, purposes and values. In brief a human being is a person not an automaton (p. 230).

In her work Stone draws a useful distinction between one's thought patterns and one's behaviour. She suggests that it is illogical to assume that the latter always follows the former.

> Ways of behaving are mediated by factors outside the individual's control; ways of thinking may not be. An individual may feel very

> worthy but know that employment affects well over half of all black school leavers in parts of London. However worthy he/she may feel about himself or herself as an individual, as a worker he or she knows that his or her future (work) behaviour is largely outside his or her control (p.229).

Stone concludes that:

> The (normal) self-concept of black children and adults is therefore best understood in terms of the development of a culture which acts to protect and sustain the individual and the group. 'Culture' in this sense is taken to mean the values and world view of the group as shown in languages, dialect, literature, music, religious and political movement which historically reflect the striving for individual and group autonomy (p.234).

Resistance as a conscious strategy

Macro-sociological terminology which states that racism oppresses black people, and similarly that sexism oppresses women and capitalism oppresses the working class, may fail to allow space for the unpicking of the micro-sociological dimension, the interactionist view, the individual's own interpretation of their experience. Jackie remembers her school experiences and how she was conscious of her relationship with her teacher:

> I found that a lot of teachers were sympathetic to me. They didn't really understand what was going on inside me but she behaves well, she's quiet. They were all very nice, I mean uniformly nice to me.

These quotes from the life history subjects may help us to appreciate to what extent these individuals negotiated and interpreted their individual educational experiences within an 'oppressive' society. Jackie was aware of the negative environment but she was able to respond to it positively:

> I think it's a case of getting to know who you are and being able to convince yourself that even if other people reject you, you still have a sense of identity. I think even more towards the 'O' level stage that it began to happen a lot more. I became baptised when I was about 16. I think that had a great effect on my academic work as well, because it gave me even more motivation to do well for another reason.

She continued,

> Unless you get to the point where you stop and start to be rational you are going to be destroyed by the whole thing. You are going to be so involved in counteracting the racism that you encounter in a negative way that you are going to destroy yourself with hatred. You are going to destroy your chances of getting anywhere in school.

The role of self-discipline as an adaptive strategy was central to the experience of these respondents. Their refusal to live up to negative stereotypes and their perceptive responses to blatant provocation ensured a proactive rather than reactive response to racist behaviour.

Religion reverses status frustration

In Calley's (1965) exploration of black Pentecostal churches, he framed a tentative hypothesis that adherence to emotional and puritanical religious groups was, in part, compensation for rejection by the national majority. He viewed church members as having a purpose in life which enables them to feel superior to those who look down on them. However, Calley asserts that the 'withdrawal from society' could be viewed as a negative feature in that church members rejected societal values.

> Success in this world is almost synonymous with pride and devotion to the devil; lack of worldly success is the badge of the saint (p.6).

Not one of the life history subjects — religious or non-religious — concurred with Calley's analysis. On the contrary, these individuals gave evidence of their religion offering them 'positive strokes' which led to self-esteem and self-confidence and the emotional energies to take on the challenges of self-development. Jason said:

> One of the things which being Christian has meant for me is that I've started to work in finding the positive things about myself and that has been a real turnaround. It takes quite a few years to be able to overcome a lot of the negatives which have been reinforced by society. Everything like school. To get to the point where I don't care what the people say because I know who I am, what I am, where I am coming from and where I am going. Some people might say that religion is a crutch but as far as I am concerned it has helped me where other people have failed and it has helped me to be myself despite the efforts of almost all society.

If Calley's references to worldly success are taken to mean monetary success, his contribution could indeed inform our discussion. For although Weber's (1971) thesis on protestantism's role in capitalism cannot be ignored, other aspects of sectarian philosophy discourage the 'cut and thrust' and ruthlessness deemed to be integral to enterprise and profit making.

The respondents who were currently church members stated clearly that their relationship with God, that sense of knowing that he was ultimately in charge of the working out of their 'career path', gave them confidence. That he was able to put in motion anything for their good or defend them from any negative experience left them reassured about their present circumstances and optimistic about their future. An appreciation of the purpose of 'suffering' or 'disappointments' was central to their understanding of God's way of working. They knew that their lives would not be without problems but they were confident that allowing God lead through even the most difficult circumstances would ultimately be a means of strengthening their character — thus making them more 'Christ-like'. Amanda explains her understanding of this acceptance:

> It makes you see that there can always be positive outworkings. Sometimes I have real problems and I can talk to God about it. I ask what is going on? Why have you put me here? Why have I got to be confronting all this?

Respondents who had been brought up as members of a sect but were not currently active members, admitted that their overt, conscious communicating with God was not as regular as in their childhood. However, they expressed appreciation of the character-building their religious upbringing had provided. They described a subconscious reserve of inner strength on which they could call in times of difficulty. Nick said:

> I couldn't say I'd turn round and say God help me and sustain me through that. But I think it helps in the resilience that you display. A kind of inner hardness that says there are trials and tribulations but you must keep hammering at them. In that kind of abstract, covert way, yes it helped.

This chapter has examined in some depth the accounts of experiences which relate to the respondents' religious upbringing. Chapters four, five and six have focused on the life history subjects' perception of experiences and events in their lives. In an attempt to examine the possible links between the experiences of the individuals who were interviewed for this research project and other black people, Chapter seven uses other biographical and historical material to explore the function and dysfunctional role religion is said to play in the lives of other black people.

Chapter 7

Black people and religion — a wider view

The past three chapters have focused on the life history material collected in a local area. The individuals were members of the black communities in and around Sheffield. During the conversations the subjects presented the benefits they perceived religion having brought into their lives. They also shared with me their views on the ways in which religion was used by black people throughout history. They noted the role played by belief systems in the lives of groups of people who were experiencing oppress-ion. Amanda said:

> Black people have often used religion to help them cope with racism and other forms of oppression. In America in the 1960s black people sang hymns and negro spirituals such as 'We shall overcome', 'My God is real', 'What a morning', 'Good news', 'He's got the whole world in his hand', to comfort themselves and boost their self-worth. These songs were composed during slavery. The Rastafarians use religious ideas to help them cope with 'Babylon', Muslims and other religious groups of black people use religion to protect and defend themselves from the worst aspects of western racist European behaviour.

This chapter examines the views expressed by Amanda and other respondents. In the foreshadowing ideas that inspired this study I considered the specific role of religion in the lives of African-Caribbean achievers in the British education system. More general observations had also led me to reflect on the possible historical patterns which might underpin and mirror local events. The previous chapters only briefly note expressions of dissatisfaction with the views and practices of black churches in Britain. So far, a positive, functional role of religion has largely been promoted in the study. A closer look at indications of the dysfunctional, negative uses of religion would provide a more balanced account.

A historical contextualisation of this work appeared to be one way of assessing the claims and counter-claims concerning the ambivalent role of religion in relation to dealing with racial oppression. Biographical material about black leaders reveals similarities and differences in the ways they utilise religion in their own understanding of racial oppression. In what follows I present the biography of one black leader who appeared to lean on religious philosophies to sustain his self-esteem in the face of overt racial and social injustice. In order to broaden the discussion, I also draw on the life experiences of other historical black figures.

Whenever possible, the themes used to analyse and unpick the lives of the subjects will be used, implicitly or explicitly, in the examination of the one historical figure. Although education an aspect of social mobility, was the major focus of the earlier chapters, this chapter will consider the broader notions of social mobility.

Martin Luther King grew up in an area where racism was a prevailing social injustice and where black people had suffered discrimination for decades. He came to the forefront of the struggle for civil rights in the 1950s and remained a central figure for the rest of his life. Many people would describe him as 'the leader' of the civil rights movement in America at that time.

I am not seeking to enter into a discussion or make judgements about the political correctness of the historical figures discussed here. Considerable discussions can be found elsewhere about their involvement with party politics at national and international levels. Judgements have been and are being made about the effectiveness and tactics of black political leaders. This is not the place for the unpicking of these debates. Similarly, opposing views about the role of leaders can be found in sociological literature. On the one hand, the very concept of leadership implies the proposition that individuals can make a difference to historical events — a proposition has never really been universally accepted. A brief discussion of concept of leadership may be helpful at this stage. Shuker (1988) remarks that:

> From classical times to the present day, eminent thinkers have regarded individuals as no more than the agents and pawns of larger forces, whether the gods, goddesses of the ancient world or, in the modern era, race, class, nation, the dialectic, the will of the people, the spirit of the times, history itself. Against such forces the individual dwindles into insignificance (p.9).

The place of the individual is examined in the concept of historical determinism. The thesis of determinism contends that 'the leader' is the slave of history. However, the idea of men and women as the slaves of history runs counter to the deepest human instincts. Rigid determinism abolishes the idea of human freedom and the idea of human responsibility, since it is manifestly unfair to reward or punish people for actions that are by definition beyond their control. Living consistently by any deterministic creed appears to be untenable. Therefore, history also refutes the idea that individuals make no difference. In Shuker's words:

> For better or for worse, individuals do make a difference. The notion that a people can run itself and its affairs anonymously, is now well known to be the silliest of absurdities. Individuals of genius show the way, and set the pattern, which common people then adopt and follow (p.9).

As a compromise, it could be said that leaders such as Martin Luther King cannot be effective by themselves. They must act in response to the rhythms of their age. It may be that great leaders seize the opportunities of their time, the hopes, fears, frustrations, crises and potential of their people. It could be that they succeed when events have prepared the way for them; when the community is waiting to be aroused; and when they can provide the clarifying and organising ideas. '*Leadership ignites the circuit between the individual and the mass and thereby alters history for better or for worse*' (Shuker, 1988, p.8)

Information for the life story of Martin Luther King Junior is drawn from a number of biographers, principally Shuker (1988), Schloredt and Brown (1988) and King's autobiographical writings.

Growing up with racism

Martin Luther King Junior was born in Atlanta on 15th January 1929, the third child of Albertha and Martin Luther King Senior. He was named after his father, and the family called him ML for short, a nickname that stuck (and is used in this chapter). His father was the pastor of the Ebenezer Baptist church in Atlanta. ML was an active, curious and clever boy. At five, he was memorising passages from the Bible, at six, he would sing gospel songs for the congregation. All the time he was learning. One day after hearing a guest minister give an impressive sermon, ML told his parents, '*Some day, I'm going to get me some big words like that!*' Martin and his siblings played with the neighbourhood children but, like all black children, his childhood and youth were scarred by racial prejudice. Every day, little things made it clear to him that to be black was to be a second class citizen.

One day an incident happened of the kind that many black parents of that generation dreaded. As the day approached for ML to start school, he was told by one of his friends, the son of a white merchant whose store was across the street, that they could not play together anymore because ML was black. '*He softened the news by pointing out that they would be going to different schools anyway.*' At the dinner table ML confronted his family with this bewildering development. The Kings responded by recounting to yet another black child the history of blacks in the United States, detailing the insults and injustices they were forced to suffer. '*You must never feel that you are less than anyone else*' his mother told him. '*You must always feel that you are somebody.*' Young King was greatly shocked by the history his parents unfolded for him. At that time, he later wrote, he was '*determined to hate all white people*' (Shuker, 1988).

As he grew up, Martin learned that segregation — the two races living completely separate lives — was a fact of life in the South. As a black person he could only use certain public drinking fountains and toilets; the others had signs hanging in front of them saying 'Whites Only'. If he wanted an ice cream cone, he was sent to the side window outside the shop. When he wanted to see a film, he couldn't sit downstairs. That was reserved for whites. He had to go up to the back balcony. Blacks and whites did not go to school together, or use the same public library or the same parks. Blacks never lived in white areas.

> On the one hand, my mother taught me that I should feel a sense of somebodiness. On the other hand, I had to go out and face the system which stared me in the face everyday, saying 'You are less than'. 'You are not equal to'. So there was a real tension within (Schulke *et.al.*, 1986).

> The most humiliating incident occurred when ML was 15 and in his final year of high school. He belonged to the school debating society and had gone with the society to a contest in another town, where he won a prize for his speech 'The Negro and the Constitution'. It was a proud moment, and he was feeling happy and pleased as he and his teacher rode home on the bus that night. As the bus went on, more passengers boarded, until all the seats were taken. Then two white passengers got on, and the bus driver demanded that ML and his teacher stand and give up their seats. ML refused, but the driver insisted, calling him a 'black bastard'. This made ML terribly angry. He had just been awarded a prize for his speech on black people's rights, yet here were the very same constitutional rights he had spoken about being pushed aside and forgotten. He felt like fighting, but he was with his teacher, who was frightened and begging him to stand up and avoid trouble. There was very little ML could do at that moment, so he stood up, furious at having to give in. It was one of the bitterest moments he had every known (Scholoredt and Brown, 1988), p.11).

Family Values

Besides being a minister, Reverend King was a shrewd businessman, and the family lived well. But being a minister and reasonably well-to-do meant nothing to the local white community; to them this gentle man was just another 'nigger'. But ML's father knew how to respond to insults. When a policeman stopped him on the road one day and said '*Boy, let me see your license*', the Reverend King pointed to his son and said '*See that child there? That is a boy, I am a man*'. He ran a great risk of being called 'uppity' but his son admired his courage and his dignity. He would always remember what his father said about racism: '*I don't care how long I have to live with the system. I am never going to accept it. I'll fight it till I die.*' Because he was a preacher, ML's father 'Daddy King' had an important position in the black community. The church played a vital role in the life of black people in the American South. It was the heart of inspiration and comfort for people whose lives were hard throughout the other six days of the week.

School, Higher Education experiences and doubts about the church

When ML was 15 he took an early entrance examination for Morehouse College, in Atlanta, one of the best black colleges in the country. Because World War II had drained students into the army, a special programme was set up to admit exceptional high school students. King passed the examinations but discovered, to his chagrin, that when he entered college, his 'separate but equal' public education had left him with a reading age much below the average white student.

ML's father was hoping that his namesake would follow in his career path and be a minister, but ML thought he might like to become a lawyer or a doctor. He felt that these professions would be more useful to his people.

> This was a turbulent time for him. His father clearly expected him to study for the ministry, but ML had doubts about the effectiveness of the church in helping black people to attain their civil rights. In addition he had questions about the literal interpretation of the Bible taught by the Baptist church. And, most of all, he was embarrassed by the emotional nature of his father's sermons. ML loved his father, but he did not feel he could truly follow in his footsteps. Instead his heart was set on civil rights issues (Shuker, 1988, p.10).

ML received his degree from Crozer Seminary in Chester, Pennsylvania. This was his first experience in an integrated school and he finished at the head of his class. He then won a scholarship to Boston University's School of Theology to study for his doctorate. After he was awarded the doctorate in theology he was known as 'Dr' or 'Reverend' King.

Role models and acknowledging the role of religion

ML entered Morehouse in the autumn of 1944, determined to become a lawyer. He could see no other way of helping his people break down the legal barriers that kept them from the rights of social mobility in the mainstream of American life. He could not yet defy his father openly, but he knew in his heart that his mission in life was to help end racial discrimination. The black churches, in his opinion, could not work directly for that cause.

At Morehouse ML found an answer to his conflict in his intellectual mentor, Dr Benjamin Mays. He was the president of the college and the person who most influenced ML's choice of career. Mays was a southern black man who had been educated in Chicago, been a pastor in several black churches before becoming a professor of theology and a college administrator. Mays, too, had strong feelings about the failings of the black churches in the South. He thought that they were offering their congregation relief from the pain of oppression when they should have been more concerned with opposing that oppression through social and political action. He wanted to see a renewal of social responsibility in the churches that would play a central role in improving the lives of black people.

Under Mays' influence, ML began to understand the churches' potential to stir the hearts of black people, something which politics alone might not achieve. While still at Morehouse, he told his father that he wanted to join the ministry and he studied the ideas of other theologians and philosophers. But the man whose beliefs most excited ML was Mahatma Gandhi, the Indian leader who had led his country to freedom from the political and military clutches of imperialist Britain, through non-violent resistance. Gandhi's philosophy was not passive. He believed that one must stand up to oppression and even be willing to die in the effort. But he also felt that there was more power in changing one's enemy through a love for common humanity than in reciprocating the same hate and violence.

Gandhi called this love 'Satyagraha' and with its force he mobilised the masses of the poor of India to stand up to the British and their superior weapons, technology and wealth. Gandhi promoted the dignified acceptance of their enemies as fellow human beings. King was intrigued with this notion of love. He knew it was not the same as the love one felt for friends or the love between husband and wife. He discovered that the ancient Greeks had a special word for this kind of love, *Agape*, which meant redeeming goodwill for all humanity. To King it was the same love that Christianity taught. When Christ said to love thine enemy, King thought, *agape* was exactly what he meant.

In his youth, Martin had agonised about the potential of the black church to progress the quest for social equality. Later in his career he was confident of the contribution the black church could play. He was not, however, uncritical of the institution or the growing affluent black individuals within it. In his own words:

> Two types of negro churches have failed to provide bread. One burns with emotionalism and the other freezes with classism. The former, reducing worship to entertainment, places more emphasis on volume than on content and confuses spirituality with muscularity. The danger in such a church is that the members may have more religion in their hands and feet than in their hearts and souls. At midnight this type of church has neither the vitality nor the relevant gospel to feed hungry souls. The other type of negro church that feeds no midnight traveller has developed a class system and boasts of its dignity, its membership of professional people, and its exclusiveness (King, 1963, p.22).

King felt that these 'black puritans' who had achieved success were concerned about their civil disabilities rather than the vast mass of their people who were desperate, poor and still hopelessly near to slavery. Such concerns were founded on evidence that these church members were more philanthropic than revolutionary. Despite accusations of escapism, King was articulate about the active responsibility of the church rather than a false other worldliness. He stated:

> I'm not concerned with the temperature of hell, or the furnishings of heaven, but with the things men do here on earth... there are still too many negro churches that are so absorbed in a future good 'over yonder' that they condition their membership to adjust to present evils 'over here' (King, 1968, p.23).

Being awarded the Nobel Peace Prize in 1964 made it clear that the world community respected and applauded Martin Luther King's attempts and achievements in the sphere of improving human relations. A great number of black people in the southern states of America supported his views, responding to his calls for boycotts and marches. However King was severely criticised by a number of black leaders who objected to his philosophy and his approach. Lewis (1970), a young black historian, stated that he had never been stirred by the personality or the non-violent doctrine of Martin Luther King.

> He remains, for me, essentially a Baptist preacher whose extraordinary rhetorical abilities were not quite matched by practical intelligence and political radicalism (p.28).

Others suggested that his work was irrelevant and obstructive, since he provided for the oppressive white system an attractive alternative to the uncompromising attitudes of individuals like Malcolm X and Elijah Muhammad. On a wider, more debatable scale, other critics suggested that by sentimentalising and almost idolising King, Christians were retreating from reality and thereby hindering the revolution needed to bring about social justice within and among nations. These critics observe the power of the mass media communication to promote a personality. They underline the philosophy which leads to the creation of an appealing contemporary hero. They deny that King's approach to social injustice could have any real and lasting significance.

It appears to many who analysed this period that in the struggle for equality, the black church played an ambivalent role. On the one hand it could be described as the first of the black community's free institutions that had been permitted for black people under slavery. It was not a counterpart to the white man's church but was the only setting where tradition could be sustained:

> It was the sole repository of tradition, the conservatory of the Afro-American musical heritage, the seed-bed of every emerging social concern, of faith, literacy and education (Lewis, p.17).

On the other hand the black people of America in the 1950s and 1960s had just cause to regard the church with a degree of suspicion. Some argue that because it was the only institution permitted in the days of slavery; its character had been one of compromise and caution. However much it was the 'seed-bed of every emerging social concern', the expression of those concerns was bound to be muted by the whole ethos of the church and its message. That ethos, it was suggested, was predominantly escapist, centred not upon change but upon compensation. The future life of joy for suffering borne in this world was its central theme. 'Steal away to Jesus', a regularly sung spiritual, indicated a religion of social and political withdrawal, rather than engagement.

The advocates of black power suggested that King was a deluded idealist; they viewed his tactics as misguided and counter-productive. Lewis (1970) observes that:

> With superb courage and high faith, ML King marched his men, like the Grand Old Duke of York, up the hill and down again for years, but it was the firing of the Negro ghettos which rocked Capitol Hill on its foundations. Doors that King and his followers had knocked upon suddenly yielded to the hefty kick of Negro militancy (Lewis, p.12).

In his fight to dismantle racial segregation and secure constitutional rights for black Americans, Dr King found direction and guidance from his religion. For him religion legitimated and nourished his demands for changes within the given political structure.

Unlike Dr King, other black leaders have utilised religion to justify a more radical and uncompromising response to white suppression. By briefly looking at one such black leader we can see how Marxist views can be merged with religious views to complement rather than condemn or criticise each other. Smith and Simpson (1981) in their biography of Robert Mugabe, describe him as an influential and articulate but reluctant leader in Southern Africa. As the first Prime Minister of Zimbabwe, Mugabe led his nation out of economic, social and political inequality towards self-rule and independence. A legacy of overt racism had haunted Rhodesians, with the constant memories of the bigoted empire-builder Cecil Rhodes when their country still carried his name.

Most of Mugabe's early education was by Jesuit priests in Kutama. His family is described as being 'imbued with Christianity' (Smith and Simpson, p. 11). Mugabe himself valued the self-discipline and moral structure that was offered by the Church. In fact, during his bitter period of political imprisonment, he regarded education and religion as his main outlets. The refusal of permission for temporary release from prison to attend the funeral of his baby son and the wilful neglect that led to the death of his friend Takawira, were just two instances where Mugabe's religion provided comfort. During certain periods of their lives Mugabe and his wife stopped attending church but, as his biographers note,

> that doesn't mean the church had waned in its influence on them both... Mugabe recognises even today that the church first taught him the equality of man, regardless of race, in the eyes of God (Smith and Simpson, 1981, p.39).

Mugabe saw what he understood to be socialism 'in action' in Kutama and concluded,

> Because of that, and ever since then, it has always been my firm belief that socialism has to be more Christian than capitalism (Smith and Simpson, 1981, p.15).

His political speeches were peppered with religious influences. He described Mrs Thatcher as being *'in concubinage with Satan* (South African Prime Minister) *Botha*' (p.150).

Like Dr King, Mugabe felt a deep attraction to the non-violent movement as advocated by Gandhi. But for Mugabe the obvious link between Christianity and the fundamental principles of Marx legitimated radical changes in political structures where this was necessary to ensure equality. From a Marxist perspective, Mugabe understood that poverty in a capitalist society can only be understood in terms of inequality generated by a capitalist economy. Wealth is concentrated in the hands of a minority, while the majority must sell their labour in return for wages. For him, true Christianity and Marxism rejected this form of social and economic oppression. Other Christian Marxists (Scarge and Sookhedo, 1981) examine the roots of poverty and they too find the answer in the world economic system.

There is an apparent conflict between traditional Marxian notions of religion and the views of Mugabe and other Christians regarding the potential role of religion. From a Marxist perspective, religion is viewed as an element of social control which disempowers and oppresses the poor. Marx said that:

> Religion is the sigh of the oppressed creature, the sentiment of a heartless world and the soul of soulless conditions. It is the opium of the people (Haralambos, 1980, p.460).

Lenin described religion as: 'a kind of spiritual gin in which the slaves of capital drown their human shape and their dreams to any decent life (Haralambos, 1980, p.460).

From a Marxist viewpoint there are a number of ways in which religion dulls the pain of oppression, Haralambos (1980) lists four. By offering promises of an eternal bliss and paradise after death, Christianity is regarded as making life on earth more bearable. Secondly, the precept contained in Matthew 3:7 ('It is easier for a camel to pass through the eye of a needle, than for a rich man to enter the Kingdom of Heaven') advocates that the godly must bear the deprivation of poverty with dignity and humility. By making a virtue of their suffering, Christians become reluctant to demand justice in this life. The hope of supernatural intervention as a method of solving problems here on earth is offered as a third way in which religion can make life more bearable for the poor. Anticipation of future salvation, too, can make oppression more bearable. If the lower strata of society sincerely believe that God has created or ordained the social structure they may regard social arrangements as inevitable. Words of hymns such as:

> The rich man in his castle,
> The poor man at his gate,
> God made them high and lowly,
> And ordered their estate ('All Things Bright and Beautiful')

could help those at the bottom of a socially stratified system to accept and come to terms with their situation. In these ways are religious people seen to be philosophically rationalising the inevitability of their social position.

The Marxist view extends the argument by referring to religion as something which 'dulls the pain' and also the instrument of the pain. Haralambos summarised the views as follows:

> By providing explanations and justifications for social systems, religion distorts reality. It helps to produce a false class consciousness which blinds members of the subject class to their true situation and their real interests. In this way it diverts attention from the real source of their oppression and so helps to maintain ruling class power (p.131).

Communists would point to population groups throughout world history where this dysfunctional role of religion was clearly evident (eg the caste system in India is justified by Hindu religious beliefs). It is clear that neither Dr King's not Mugabe's use of their religious experiences and/or affiliations fits neatly into a Marxist notion of that which can dull the pain of the oppressed. Black leaders such as Mugabe and King appear to have provided for their nations an understanding of the latent potential of religion to legitimate social equality.

Dr King's congregation might have joined in the singing of well-known gospel songs such as:

Some glad morning when this life is over
I'll fly away
To a home on God's celestial shore
I'll fly away

Refrain

Oh I'll fly away, oh glory
I'll fly away
When I die, Alleluia, by and by
I'll fly away

Just a few more weary days and then
I'll fly away
To a home where joy shall never end
I'll fly away

These words would have offered some comfort for the crude, heartless experiences endured because of racial segregation. However their belief in future salvation need not have precluded their present demand for constitutional rights. Other hymns, bible verses and sermons would have reminded them of God's belief in justice for his earthly children. Martin Luther King said:

> If segregation (were not a sin against God) the white south would not be haunted as it is by a deep sense of guilt for what it has done to the Negro — guilt for patronising him, degrading him, brutalising him, depersonalising him, thingifying him; guilt for lying to itself. This is the source of the schizophrenia that the south will suffer until it goes through its crisis of conscience (Shuker, 1988, p.42).

By believing in God's justice, Dr King and his followers could take on the task of fighting for their rights in the knowledge that they had divine assistance.

To extend traditional Marxist analysis — which omits a racial dimension — to a framework which *can* be used by black communities, Hall (1989) examines the place of religion in black British communities and the Caribbean from a structural functionalist perspective. Hall points out the value perceived by the congregations in both settings of the pastoral role and 'caring' services offered by the church. Hall remains critical of the extent to which religious organisations appear reluctant to take up the collective struggle against structural oppression in various forms and racial oppression in particular. Like Marx, he regards religion as a 'buffer' which placates and consoles oppressed peoples, thus disabling the will to rebel.

At first glance it appears that Hall 's ideas about religion are the exact opposite of the life history subjects' views. For, while they identify the enabling and empowering aspects of their belief systems, Hall stresses how their belief systems disempower and disable black people from resisting and challenging oppression. Could it be that Hall and the subjects are referring to different styles and forms of resistance and challenge? Hall (1989) is evidently concerned with overt political challenges to racist and oppressive systems. He identifies the need for black individuals to use existing local and central political channels to expose and reverse injustices which pervade all aspects of society. In conjunction with this he recognises the need for radical and militant subversive attacks on systems which are central to the oppression of black people. Hall's challenges refer principally to organised and collective forms of resistance and challenge.

The differing views on the relevance of religion to black people's political and social uprising have been discussed in other geographic and historical settings. Historical research shows that across time and continents, black people have experienced oppression: the Maoris in New Zealand, the Aborigines in Australia, Native American Indians in North America, the plunder and exploitation of the African continent. Many historical analyses of the experiences of black people begin from the period of slavery and colonialisation. The acknowledgement that 'Africans existed before slavery' suggests that an examination of the role of religion in precolonial societies would be important for comparative purposes. From this information we could access the extent to which these systems of beliefs have survived and if there is any evidence for the view that Africans adapted their traditional systems of belief to western European concepts. The fusion of religious beliefs would need to be seen in the light of the traumatic disruption suffered by the Africans. Such an examination is a thesis in itself and cannot be undertaken here.

Writers such as Lashley (1986) suggest that Caribbean islands display differences in their ability and willingness to challenge oppressive structures. These differences appear to correlate with the religious persuasions of the Europeans who colonised their islands in the 16th and 17th centuries. Islands like Jamaica, which was colonised by Protestants, appear to be more prepared to challenge the oppressive structures which aimed to destroy their lives. Whereas islands which were colonised by practising Roman Catholics appear less likely to resist and challenge their oppressive masters. Pinkney (1972) traces the development of the beginning of black Christianity. He looks at the problems the negro slaves encountered as they adopted the white man's religion.

Although he generally suggests that the church historically has played a small part in the revolution for black liberation, he notes that several major slave revolts were initiated by black ministers. There is evidence to suggest that the most militant leadership for blacks came from the clergy:

> A few notable examples are Henry Highland Garnet, a Presbyterian minister to a white congregation, who urged slaves to kill any slaveholder who refused to release them. Henry M. Turner, the militant bishop of the African Methodist Episcopal church, who championed the cause of black repatriation to Africa and who was the first to teach that 'God is a negro'. George Alexander McGuire, who left the Episcopal church to head Marcus Garvey's African Orthodox church. Adam Clayton Powell, the long-term Congressman from New York's Harlem and the first convener of the first black power conference in 1966 (Pinkney, 1972, p.152).

Pinkney also cites the activities of Dr Martin Luther King and Jessie Jackson.

There is some evidence to support the Marxist view of the role of religion in society. There is also plenty of evidence which contradicts it. An examination of the role of religion in the life experiences of black people suggests that a traditional Marxist analysis cannot be applied.

In the concluding chapter of the book I will continue to probe the subjects' predominantly positive views about religion. I will also consider areas which have been neglected or ignored in the main body of the study.

Chapter 8

Implications for education

The previous chapters have covered a number of wide ranging issues. Religion, education and the subjective reality of the respondents have been core themes. These themes have mushroomed, reaching their roots deep into related fields.

This concluding discussion attempts to draw the disparate themes together. For the sake of clarity, it is organised into four sections.

My experiences of postgraduate study;

The possible fragmenting of the African-Caribbean community;

The current and future position of the black church, and

The role of welfare institutions in the lives of black people.

By reflecting on my experiences and perceptions of writing this study I may observe patterns similar to those of the educational experiences of the respondents. The respondents' varied comments about their relationships with other church members and their adherence to religious philosophies casts some light on the current and possible future position of black sects. The black community in Britain has never been a homogeneous whole. Yet, as each generation finds roots and 'settles' into Britain as its home, it may be that a natural process of fragmentation of the community will occur. Respondents, especially those who have white partners, reflected on the possible consequences of this potential disintegration. Throughout the project, respondents described the negative experiences in schools, colleges and other education establishments. A brief examination of black people's experiences of other 'welfare institutions' is relevant to the examination of the position of black people in Britain.

My reflections and observations

Being 'part-time'

Embarking on what was to be a PhD thesis was, with hindsight, a brave (or foolish) enterprise. Having two young children, a full-time job, community and domestic responsibilities demanded a high degree of personal organisation. Rita's (in Chapter four) description of her mother 'juggling balls' is one I can relate to and empathise with. However the opportunity to undertake this exciting and, for many in the black community, highly relevant project could not be missed. Two years previously I had commenced a part-time Masters degree. Illness related to early months of pregnancy brought this to a premature conclusion. I enjoyed the mental stimulation and academic rigour of the course but found that much of the content lacked a sense of personal relevance. To some extent it appeared inconsequential, unlike the central themes of the study.

Self-questioning about my own community's position in society had gripped my attention for many years. Explanations and analysis offered by professional or academics had always seemed to me to be incomplete. But without access to certain academic tools, resources and structure, an in-depth exploration of certain questions seemed unavailable. For the concluding components of my first degree I chose to discuss issues relating to 'West Indian children in British Schools'. My terminology and emphasis reflected the socio-political thinking of the time. Referring to black British children as 'West Indian' indicated my lack of political awareness or possibly a reluctance to challenge the terminology in use at that time. So as political and social awareness developed I yearned for an opportunity to examine other related issues.

Dr Breinberg took a personal interest in me. Speaking as an academic working in the university and as a friend, she declared a personal and professional interest in my ideas. Her involvement in helping me to secure the postgraduate place was invaluable. Like Rita's Mrs A, and Nick's teacher, Dr Breinberg's knowledge of the academic system coupled with her belief in my latent abilities, paved the way for my place at the university. Although she now lives thousands of miles from me, at the southern-most part of the North American continent, my mother has been a steady 'force' driving me towards the ultimate conclusion of this project. She has been the driving force behind much of the academic progress of my sister (Barrister at law LLM) and myself.

Being a part-time postgraduate student at the university has been an experience which has evoked many emotions. Early feelings of enthusiasm for the subject and the opportunity to generate new ideas were often stifled by a sense of unbelonging or being out of place. Locating other black colleagues and white who were interested in these issues and building a network of mutual support proved to be a vital lifeline. Feeling 'dismissed', usually by senior male white colleagues, could then be discussed in a supportive setting. The sheer process of being a part-time student with other commitments has to be lived to be believed. It was the 'little' inconveniences that sometimes almost broke the 'researcher's back'. Not having access to a word-processor on the university site proved to be a time-consuming inconvenience. Only recently finding out that a postgraduate area existed where one could leave piles of books in a locker left me with feelings of annoyance and embarrassment, as I inevitably had to walk around with 'shopping bags' full of books.

The tension of divided loyalties between domestic responsibilities and being a student has never subsided. Those who examine the traumas of working mothers identify the personal and practical difficulties which must be dealt with before progress is possible. Becker (1986) points to differing strategies that men and women use to prepare themselves emotionally for research and writing. These activities could be seen as magical rituals or neurotic symptoms. Women commonly found they were 'compelled' to clean the house before they could start their writing; men were more likely to sharpen twenty pencils! I find it very difficult to miss parents' evenings at school or 'neglect' getting the children to after school classes. Carving out time for myself has felt selfish. The subject area being discussed has obviously influenced my responses to my own children's education, but studying in the late evening or at nights, whether inside or outside the home, have their own difficulties. Women have been attacked in certain areas of Sheffield during late evenings and at night. On the other hand I find that being at home makes me too available for others. The university library is certainly not the proverbial 'cabin in the woods' but it was usually the most peaceful place I could find to think through my ideas or the subject in hand.

Oh, how I envied those students who were able to use the library all day and every day. Working consistently without distractions seemed idyllic. When I began the thesis my motivation was personal interest in exploring a range of ideas. This optional dimension has now been overtaken by the pressure to research and publish, as a senior lecturer in higher education. Having the opportunity to study at postgraduate level as a part-time student is an obvious advantage when substantial funding for such a project is so unlikely. I had no option but to examine the issues as a part-time student.

Choosing the subject

From the outset I was clear that the subject area needed careful handling from a personal and community perspective. As a black Christian who is an active member of one of the sects discussed in the thesis (Seventh-Day Adventist) and who is also currently teaching and studying in a Higher Education establishment, my cultural, religious and emotional affinity to the work required constant assessment. It is likely that my personal belief in the philosophy of Adventism sometimes impeded my objectivity and could encourage emotionalism which might be communicated, implicitly rather than overtly. On occasions I had to reflect on the possibility or respond to concerns that the thesis could be regarded as an evangelical exposition. I had to be conscious of these eventualities and constantly guard against them. Discussing the subject with non-Christians as well as non-church members helped to provide and maintain a balanced approach.

From a community perspective there were several issues that had to be considered when writing a work which could impact on the individual and collective lives of black communities. The need to preserve anonymity and yet present a fully rounded picture of each subject has been a source of creative tension. Exposing or abusing the confidences of individuals in such a small sample could have been counter-productive to the aims of the thesis. Whatever research benefits were to be gained from ignoring the specific subjects' requests could not be deemed to be worthwhile if the 'trust' placed in the researcher was seen to be misplaced.

The 'trust' of the black community could have been more tangentially destroyed if this thesis was received as a negative contribution to current political debate. Local and central government funds have for a number years been injected into African-Caribbean communities via self-help projects, staffing for social services departments, education departments and various building projects. The basis for much of this funding has been the acknowledgement that disadvantage, discrimination and racism has a negative impact on the lives of black people. This thinking has generated funds for various developments such as the Sheffield and District African-Caribbean Association, and the Sheffield United Multiracial Education Service. These organisations are given funds and accommodation which should be used to redress the impact of oppressive forces. Research findings such as those central to the thesis, which question the assumption that black people are inevitably the victims of racism, could be seen as a threat to funding.

More than this, any suggestions that black individuals are personally responsible for the resulting impact of racism will, rightly, be refuted. Whether the thesis has adequately balanced the need to highlight the (individual and collective) strengths of the communities and their ability to resist the ravages of racism when it is of such a pervasive and endemic nature, is debatable. It was not intended to be regarded as ammunition or an escape route for politicians and educators whose rhetoric about anti-racism rarely match their actions. Although I obviously hope that 'conventional wisdom' concerning black children in British schools will be challenged, none of the ideas presented here should be used to dilute the thrust towards equal opportunity or the fight against racism. Being cognizant of those highly relevant but possibly conflicting ideas was just the beginning. To complete the thesis I had to 'master the skill' of presenting a range of ideas on paper.

'Writing' — work or play?

The basic skills of the English language was made available to me in primary and junior schools. During my secondary education they were sharpened and certain errors were pointed out during my undergraduate years. I won a story competition in my teens but had never regarded myself as having a talent for communicating ideas orally or on paper. The writing of the thesis presented me with several problems. Using the literature, choosing the methodology and ordering the chapters are three of the main issues I faced once I started 'to write'. I feel that one fundamental factor underpinned these and other 'problems' I faced. After discussing the three areas I will offer some thoughts on the underlying factor which may have contributed to my difficulty.

The literature

Reading the literature around the pertinent and more tangential areas of the thesis was an enjoyable activity as it gave depth and breadth to areas of personal interest. On the other hand, Becker's (1986) warning about being 'terrorised by the literature' vividly describes some of my, and other more seasoned researchers' responses to well-established material. The advice from Becker to '*use the literature rather than allowing it to use you*', is sound and timely. He comments:

> The feeling that you can't say what you mean in the language you are using will warn you that the literature is crowding you. It may take you a long time to find out that this has happened to you (p.149).

Feeling compelled to find alliances with eminent authors in your related fields of study is possibly among the basic needs of any researcher. Being in some way original is a fundamental requirement of research. Therefore:

> No one wants to discover that their carefully nurtured idea was in print before they thought of it (maybe before they were born) and in a place where they should have looked... Students want to show the world, and all the critics who may be out there lying in wait for them, that they have looked and that no one has had their idea before (Becker, 1986, p.136).

I searched high and low, in obvious and not so obvious places, for written discussions on the core themes of the thesis. I had access to oral discussions with interested work colleagues and others in the black community. After a long and largely futile search through libraries, I am fairly sure that the prerequisite of originality is present in this thesis. Once I was clear about the set of ideas that needed to be shared, the next stage was to find the correct form for presentation. Using Durkhiem, Weber or other well established sociologists seemed inevitable if my work was to be deemed to be theoretically sound. However, the temptation to use their language as well as their ideas required constant vigilance. My own style often seemed 'woolly' compared to the precision and neat structure of the 'masters' and often led to severe writer's block. Overcoming this dilemma came over time, as my sense of confidence developed.

Organising and ordering the ideas

Once I had made a 'final' decision on the merits of the chosen methodological approach, arranging the ideas so that they formed a logical and convincing argument was crucial. For example, my foreshadowing ideas had located religion as a very significant factor. But I was tempted to allow the religious theme to seep out of the transcripts, thus leaving more detailed discussion of its role in black people's lives till much later in the thesis. I wrestled with the merits of a chapter which opened up a critical examination of the sociology of religion. Although this was not undertaken, sociological concepts informed and influenced my thinking throughout. I wondered whether I should have allowed the reader (examiner) to imbibe the views of the subject before presenting information about the sect they belonged to.When I decided the order of the final work, I gave due consideration to the need for a logical monograph which would accomodate the readers' lack of specific knowledge.

A combination of problems seemed to arise out of trying to get everything right at once and this often caused what seemed to be terminal cases of writer's block. Not all these problems have been completely resolved. Yet a growing sense of confidence has allowed me to complete the thesis. Finally getting the thesis 'out of the door' has been a tremendous motivating factor. The tension between getting it better and getting it done was largely resolved by deadlines. The temptation to hold on to a chapter or the whole script until I had found a better way of expressing my ideas was almost overwhelming. Becker (1986) pointed out that this malaise is not restricted to those who are new to research or to social science.

> The American composer Charles Ives just didn't care, in the later stages of his composing career, whether anything ever got out the door. His reputation rests on works he never considered completed.

> In fact, little of his music would have been played, had not determined players bullied and wheedled until he reluctantly let them have the scores (p.123).

Becker refers to various 'types of doors' through which the work must 'exit' before its final departure from the researcher's hands. An earlier level would be discussion with interested peers, while the final exit would be submission for external examination. To balance out this encouraging piece of advice, Becker advocated 'getting it out' and 'waiting a while' as mottos for budding writers *both* being suitable. I think I have heeded both pieces of advice!

Finally I have come to understand that to some extent I have a 'creative child' (Nelson, 1985) inside who can create ideas on a page if given the emotional and physical space to do so. The self-recriminations and guilt that have haunted the writing of this thesis have caused many forms of writer's block. As with a number of the subjects, the ghost of childhood experiences of education need to be exorcised. By completing and submitting this thesis I have taken what seems to be only the first step in research. Using the ideas of others about solving methodological and other difficulties in writing is essential. But just as getting in the water is the only way to begin swimming lessons, so taking the risk to offer my ideas is an inevitable first stage.

Central to my experiences as outlined above and in Chapter three, is the acknowledgement and appreciation of the close-knit support structure available in the black community. It is arguable that my own experiences have led me to present an image of a cohesive, united black community. There may be a need to reassess an implied over-idealised notion of a community characterised by solidarity and mutual support. On closer observation, a researcher could observe what could be regarded as disintegrative tendencies. Certain phenomena appear to be at work which may result in a more fragmented, looser form of community. One such phenomenon which deserves examination is the growth of bi-racial intimate relationships and marriages. The social position and psychological stability of the children of such unions have recently been the source of much debate. The following section examines the potential role of black sects in what could be described as a looser community.

A fragmented community?

Up to this point the thesis has largely presented a picture of a black community which is essentially cohesive and homogeneous. Little has been said about the 'differences' and sometimes disagreements between people of different islands or nations. 'Small Island' for example is a mildly derogative term used by Jamaicans and others to refer to people from smaller islands such as Barbados and St Kitts. Differences in cultural traditions, languages and national outlooks ensure a creative tension which can sometimes cause misunderstandings and discords. Despite these underlying 'differences', as a community black British individuals find a source of strength in their need for and the making of collective responses to experiences of racism. Different levels of racial awareness and conscience-raising (Small, 1987) result in varied approaches to the oppressive forces of racism but, essentially, common strategies bind together the black community as a racially oppressed group.

Before I embarked on this work I regularly observed that significant numbers of 'famous' black people had white partners. Sports personalities eg John Barnes, musicians, comedians (eg Lenny Henry) were often seen in public with their white partners. In itself this observation was interesting.

I became increasingly interested in this apparent phenomenon as I noted how many respondents were currently with or had in the past had intimate relationships with white people. My curiosity was centred on the extent to which these black individuals, who had all at some time faced individual and institutional racism, experienced any sense of divided loyalty. Many of the respondents worked in the 'race relations industry', as advocates of racial justice and equality of opportunities. Could their personal positions in any way be seen as compromising their professional standpoints? My observations of black people in the public eye and that a significant percentage of the respondents had white partners could imply that bi-racial marriage could perhaps be class related. This is not my intention; indeed many members of the African-Caribbean community express passionate concerns about the drift of unemployed youth, especially black males, into bi-racial relationships that appear to have no prospects for social mobility. Many feel that these relationships are often the result of stereotypical notions about the virility and sexual prowess of the black man. These are interesting areas which warrant further study.

They clearly encompass a variety of psycho-social and political issues. I do not intend to unravel aspects of 'dual race' relationships here — it could be a thesis in itself.

Respondents spoke about how, as students in polytechnics and universities, friendships were obviously developed with a wide selection of individuals. 'Race' was often a factor which shaped the students' experiences, as Rita discovered (see Chapter four). She felt excluded from the friendship groups of the white students and was treated as if she were a novelty. Others spoke of the breadth of friends they acquired as a group who studied and socialised together. Union events at universities and polytechnics were organised for students to relax and have 'deserved' recreation after hours of study. Before the Conservative government reduced student grants, fewer students had to take jobs for the purpose of basic maintenance. Some were able to afford social events and travel, which afforded them the time and space to develop and share views and opinions. During such interactions students eventually — maybe inevitably — form personal attachments. The flip side of student life also created opportunities for building relationships. Many students find their vulnerable and apparently powerless position stressful. Mutual support and sharing is often integral to student relationships. Many close and intimate relationships are the outcomes of differing pressures and the ambience of full-time undergraduate study.

An extensive discussion of the correct terminology to describe children whose parents are from different 'races' can be found elsewhere (Small et al, 1986, Ahmed, 1985, Wilson, 1987). I will use a selection of different terms which I regard as contributing to the breadth of the discussion. The well-established and current literature which examines the experience of bi-racial children in Britain emphasises almost exclusively the social isolation, psychological crises and personal sufferings of this group. Much of this debate is to be found in social work literature, as 'mixed parentage' children are over-represented in the national statistics of children who are under the care of social services departments. There is no consensus in the literature on the long-term social and psychological position of many of these children. But the current prevailing view of 'dual-race' children is that they are likely to have identity problems because of their apparently ambiguous social position. Subjects who were now in long-term relationships with white partners openly contemplated how best to provide support and security for their 'bi-racial' children. It is said that where one parent is black and one white, the children are bound to suffer from divided loyalty. They are seen as belonging simultaneously to both races and yet to neither. Suggestions vary about how the potential identity conflict of these children can be resolved. The crude options are to be black, to be white or to be forever pulled between the two. Most recent literature (eg *Colour of Love*, 1992) argues strongly that despite their 'dual-race' parentage, children of such unions have no option other than to see themselves as black, because white communities would not accept them.

Discussions and studies which examine the root of such attitudes (Hernton, 1969, Milner, 1975, Wilson, 1987, Alibhai-Brown and Montague, 1992) pinpoint the racist, pseudo-scientific eugenic theories which, although academically refuted, remain at the root of strident racial bigotry. This work does not allow close examination but the future of such relationships in multiracial Britain deserves further examination. The drive towards the 'melting pot' society of the 1960s has obviously failed to secure a society of racial harmony. Indeed people of 'bi-racial' parentage describe society as more an 'inferno' than a 'melting pot'.

Respondents were concerned about how to protect and support their vulnerable offspring against negative labelling based on assumptions of racial conflict. They were anxious lest their white partners might not be able or willing to accept that developing a strong, black racial identity would be essential. They worried also that their choice of partner might invite socio-political and personal questioning from community members about their commitment to the struggle against racism.

These fundamental and problematic issues caused a number of the respondents personal conflict which, they feared, might damage their relationships. The subjects who were members of churches or sects regarded their Christian views as a source of strength. They felt that their church communities were an extension of the family unit and therefore a safe haven for their children. Encouraging their children to see themselves as people who happen to be black and emphasising the humanitarian element was regarded as one way of assisting their children. Others were concerned that the neutralising of the race issue would give their children a false impression of racial harmony that denied their daily experiences of racism. They sought daily to find the balance between encouraging self-definition based on personal dignity, integrity and an appreciation of God's love for the individual, and maintaining a strong racial identity which would prepare the children for the reality of racism.

The thesis has not examined the nature and consequence of this personal conflict in the lives of a number of respondents. To some extent it has assumed that the black community, as a cohesive group, has identified strategies for resisting racism. The possible fragmentation of this group as it moves from 'immigrant' status to integration or assimilation has not been sufficiently addressed. Writers like Price (1979) have looked at different life-styles of 'West Indians' as they become assimilated to and adjusted to the British way of life. Further research obviously needs to explore the role of religion in the lives of 'bi-racial' individuals. By identifying aspects of change in the nature of the black community, there is need to reassess the postulations about the role of the church. Given that numbers of British African-Caribbeans are now socially mobile in comparison with their parents' generation, will they look to the black church in the same way as their parents did?

Current and possible future role for black religious groups in Britain

This work was inspired by an idea that religion was central to the academic progress of many African-Caribbeans in Britain. This view was borne out as the subjects came to recall the factors which influenced their academic achievement. Having established that affiliation to black churches has been significant to the educational achievement of some of its members (Chapter five) and having noted the role religion has played in the resistance against racial oppression (Chapter two), my thesis might imply that this influence appears to be a permanent one. Subsequent researchers may examine the view that the role played by religion cannot be sustained, for it will become irrelevant as black British individuals become integral members of British society.

Tangible evidence of the fact that the black church has served the needs of the black community can be seen in the establishment of the John Loughborough School. The history of its development and the responses to it by the media tell their own story.

In the late 1960s and 1970s, many black Seventh-Day Adventist parents began to express their feelings that the educational system in

Britain was failing to give their children a fair deal. They questioned the church leadership about what could be done to enhance the academic progress of their children. The church leadership was somewhat reluctant to tackle what they saw as a difficult problem, which would put financial strain upon the church organisation. 'Agitators' among the church's black membership began looking into the possibility of a school that would cater for the needs of non-indigenous Seventh-Day Adventist children. Many questioned the apparent hesitation of the church authorities. They could see no reason why there should be a church school in Watford, while the youth in the London area were left to tackle the conflicts and racism that existed within the state education system. Many parents had attended Adventist schools in the Caribbean or knew of people who had. They believed that the philosophy of such an institution would serve to encourage and motivate their children. Scholastic achievement was not the only factor that motivated parents to push for a school in London; they were concerned also about the spiritual development of each child. Adventists believe that the coming of Christ is imminent; parents had a duty accordingly, to expose their children to the teachings of Christ. London's state schools were unable to provide such a spiritual background. The standards at these schools were seen to be in direct conflict with the standards that the parents were trying to uphold in their home setting.

A synchronised effort was made among all the local churches and, finally, the church administration bought a building in North London. It is important to note how the problem was not only isolated but dealt with in an orchestrated manner and that an established system of communication already existed within the church's community. New ideas could be channelled through representatives of the various sectors, who then challenged the church administration.

In April 1980, the John Loughborough School was opened. Parents and members of the church still talk about the sacrifices that were made by individuals to bring about this 'miracle school'.

The response of the Media

When the school opened it was inundated by reporters and researchers and received national and international coverage. The various political orientations of each newspaper cannot be analysed here but their general attitude towards the new school is revealing.

Even before the school existed the concept of an all black school was under discussion. On 20 October 1977, the *West Indian World* published an article about the West Indian Standing Conference, which concerns itself with education. This Standing Conference put forward proposals for the Education ministry to set up a black school, as a pilot scheme to see whether this would enable black children to attain higher academic levels. The idea was not received warmly in all quarters. Some argued that poor academic results were not due to racism in school; that 'if only' West Indians were as disciplined as the Asian community their children would do better in school. Others feared that,

> An all-black school will only motivate the white racist to suggest further segregational schemes before we know where we are, we would have put ourselves into a trap from which there would be no return to integration (*West Indian World*, 14 October, 1977).

Three years later, the *West Indian World* introduced the John Loughborough School to the community in an article entitled 'Blacks Lead the Way' (2 May, 1980). It did not negate the point that the school is operated by the SDA church. The writer, Yvonne Collymore, discussed the question of classification with the head of the school. In reply to her questions, the head stated that he hoped that the school would be an integrated school for children of all races, and that not all the teachers would be black. Race was not the criterion for selecting staff but it would of course recognise the need to reflect the Seventh-Day Adventist Church community — which, in the London area, is predominantly black. Encouraging spiritual development would be an intrinsic aspect of the school's curriculum. Visual aids would reflect not only white but also black society. Yvonne Collymore portrayed the headmaster as an optimistic man, quite prepared to face the issues of racism within the church and outside it.

The race and the denominational issues ran side by side as equally significant factors in many media reports. In July 1980 the *Guardian* described the school as a private, denominational school catering for the West Indian community. The *Guardian* argued that parents had a strong desire 'to have their children educated in their own faith' and reported that 'West Indian' Adventist parents recognised the failures of their children in the state schools and wanted their children to encounter the highest standards in education. They believed that Adventism was capable of providing such standards.

All the media reported the assurances by the staff and head that the school would not reject white or non-Adventist children. Some suggest that it is this failure to be more selective that may cause problems for the school (Taylor, 1992).

On 12 December 1980, Trevor Philips writing for the *Times Educational Supplement*, attempted to analyse the reasons why 'ethnic minorities' were fighting to take control of their children's education. The writer placed the John Loughborough School within the context of threatening school closures, particularly in the Haringey area. The Haringey Educational Authority was reported to be proud of their educational record and stated their intention to maintain such a record even if this meant fewer schools. Opposition factions claimed that the Council's approach would be to the detriment of pupils. Parents and teachers began campaigning for smaller schools. Philips listed the various disadvantages which worried parents and teachers, such as the placement of black children in special schools or 'sin bins'. The Council was challenged to correct these problems by reforming their overall attitudes to education service provision. They were challenged to employ more black teachers, implement a multicultural curriculum, etc. The Council responded by claiming that such transformations were too expensive. Members of the community began to ask: why not our own schools? There were, after all, Church of England schools, so was it not possible to set up a similar structure?

Three years after the school was opened (1 September, 1983), the *Daily Mirror* announced that John Loughborough could 'teach others' in education administration a 'lesson'. It reported that the results at John Loughborough were three times higher than those of the nearest comprehensive school and concluded that ministers of education should face up to the reality that John Loughborough showed what is possible.

Many other organisations for the black community sprang up during the 1970s and 80s and some of these still live on. The African-Caribbean Education Research Project, Melting Pot, and the Abeng Centre are just a few of the community projects in South London. Social and recreational centres continue to grow, along with black bookshops and record shops.

The black church provides a continuous programme for members and often for non-attenders too.

The Seventh-Day Adventist church has a history of bureaucratic know-how. From its onset it had practiced the techniques of administration necessary to co-ordinate a group of people. Some of those techniques parallel those used in ancient Judaic society. This church organisation today has an efficient network of administrative, educational, welfare and health services. Since education was important within its overall philosophy, it is perhaps unsurprising that the John Loughborough School was established.

Educational and other welfare services provided by the black churches are valued by their members. In some black Pentecostal churches young couples and single parents are given enormous help. A growing number of women continue to break through the traditional expectations of female roles, to occupy leadership positions alongside men. The need to provide youth clubs and other youth-orientated facilities has long been identified, but despite the increased quality and quantity of such provisions many young adults have abandoned their parents' Christian values for alternative life-styles. In Chapter five the non-religious respondents gave some of their reasons for their disenchantment with 'church'. Eurocentric presentation, and an apparent apathy about social and racial injustices figured strongly. Bernard (1983) concluded that certain black Christianity sects and movements appear to be succumbing to the attraction and growth of Islam. She lists the following reasons for this shift in affiliation:

> Islam's influence and reliance to the continent of Africa;
>
> Its rejection of western society in preference to the strict dictates of the Koran;
>
> A philosophy that covers all aspects of life, eg politics, child rearing, salvation;
>
> The direction and security that Islam appears to give; and
>
> Its historical impact as one of the world's leading religions.

If association with black churches does provide strategies for the resistance against racial oppression, might the church become irrelevant once such strategies have been successful for the individuals concerned? A more in-depth study would need to examine the fundamental reasons for joining or leaving particular church groupings or religious denominations.

Here, I can only refer back to the respondents. They emphasised that, for them, racial oppression was just one aspect of a much wider malaise. Their fundamental belief in the opposing forces of good and evil provided them with an explanation of the purpose of their earthly existence and God's promises for eternal life.

The belief in the life, suffering, death and resurrection of Jesus (the son of God) was central to their understanding of their own life, suffering, death and life after death. Having 'faith' in these beliefs was what gave them purpose. What the influences are that determine the depth, security or longevity of this form of 'faith' deserves a great deal of discussion. This study is unable to engage in such a debate. However as an example of how sect members relate their earthly existence to their life beyond death, I present portions of a recent sermon delivered in an Adventist Church.

A few days before the 1992 general election, an Adventist minister delivered this sermon to the congregation. He used current issues to draw pertinent analogies with the need for members of the congregation to make a personal commitment to God.

Sermon title:	The Manifesto of God's Government'
Preacher:	Pastor Ian W W Sweeney
Venue:	Caterterknowle Seventh-Day Adventist Church, Sheffield
Date:	Sabbath, April 4, 1992

Introduction I am sure that none of us here today are ignorant of the fact that next Thursday, April 9 is the date of the general election. Polling booths all around the country will be opened so that those who are eligible to vote can do so. Now the decision of who we vote for is based on many differing factors. We sometimes vote for the party our parents voted for. We vote for the party which we think will benefit us most financially. We vote for the party which offers the best prospect of leading the country out of recession. We vote for those personalities who we most like. Issues such as the National Health Service, education, taxation, constitutional reform may play a role in helping us decide who we will vote for. Most of our votes will be cast between the three main parties, the Conservatives led by John Major, the Labour party led by Neil Kinnock, and Paddy Ashdown's Liberal Democrats. I myself have listened to the party political broadcasts of each party. I have listened with interest to the debates that have raged on the air-waves between the three main protagonists. I have listened and weighed up in my own mind who I might vote for.

Does anyone want to know who I might vote for next Thursday? I might vote Conservative, someone should say 'Amen'. Who is going to join me in voting for the Conservative party next Thursday? Only the Conservatives can effectively lead this country! Amen?

It is interesting, is it not, how passions can be aroused and stirred by the politics of men. By saying that I might vote for the Conservative party some of you are now upset with me. Who is going to write to the conference to tell them you don't want a Conservative party pastor, bring in a Labour party pastor. Well let me leave in peace friends, I may vote Conservative, I may vote Labour, I may vote Liberal Democrat, I may even vote for the Monster Raving Looney Party, but I am not going to tell you who I will definitely vote for. That it is my little secret.

In helping us to decide who we should vote for, all the major parties have produced a manifesto. The manifesto of each party outlines the policies and plans for the citizens of the United Kingdom if that party is voted to power on April 9. Some of you may have no interest in politics, and will not even bother to vote on Thursday. However, you need to remember that irrespective of whether we vote or not, irrespective of whether we are interested in politics or not, whoever is voted to power on Thursday will affect our lives either for better or for worse. Someone's manifesto will have an impact on our lives.

God's Manifesto My friends, today, I need to address a far more important manifesto than that produced by either the Conservative party, Labour party, or Liberal Democrats. It is a manifesto that deals with the policies of the United Kingdom of God Almighty. This manifesto has been given to the world many centuries ago so that men, women and children might read and learn. This manifesto of the United Kingdom of God tells us not only of the politics but also of the pre-requisites for citizenship in that kingdom. The manifesto of the United Kingdom of God is otherwise known as the Bible or the Word of God.

Jesus has left us in no doubt that his manifesto needs to be followed both by the letter, and through His Spirit. Jesus said in concluding the sermon on the mount in Matthew 5:24 (KJV):

'Therefore whosoever heareth these sayings of mine, and doeth them, I will liken him unto a wise man, which built his house upon a rock.'

Jesus also said in John 8:31,32:

'If ye continue in my word, then are ye my disciples indeed; And ye shall know the truth, and the truth shall make you free.'

We may be apathetic concerning the manifesto claims of the Conservatives, Labour party and the Liberal Democrats, but we cannot afford to be apathetic concerning the manifesto of God because this manifesto determines our eternal destiny.

We may even be excited over the plans of a political party, but we need a greater excitement in this church for the Word of God. No longer should this manifesto be lying idle in our homes. No longer should this book be collecting dust on our book shelves. No longer should these manifesto pages be opened only on a Sabbath and remain closed during the week. No longer should the words remain on the printed page; now is the time for the manifesto to come alive in our lives!'

The minister then emphasised the need for regular and systematic Bible study and reminded the congregation about the central tenets of belief as presented in the Bible:

This manifesto outlines all that pertains to citizenship in the Kingdom of God. It tells mankind that he is to respect his body as the temple of God. It tells mankind that God from creation has ordained a day on which he invites us to worship Him in spirit and truth. This manifesto tells mankind of the necessity to accept Jesus Christ as Lord and Saviour and of man's need to enter into a relationship with Him by means of baptism by water and the Spirit. This manifesto does not mention Sunday as the Lord's day, nether does it mention baptism of children by sprinkling. It does not mention confession of sins to a number of doctrines and teachings Christianity holds as truth. Christians need to come back to Luther's premise of '*sola scriptura*' which is scriptures alone.

The 'letter of the law' is compared and contrasted with the 'Spirit of the law'. Love for God and other humans is underscored as paramount:

Salvation not in doctrine The Bible has been given by God to men so that lives might be changed. Doctrine is important, but doctrine does not save. Knowing what to do is very different from doing what you know. We must experience the abiding presence of the Holy Ghost in our life. The experience is based upon L.O.V.E., love. Jesus said in John 14:15, 'If ye love me, keep my commandments.' He also said in John 15:17, 'These things I command you, that ye love one another.' True discipleship according to this manifesto is not singly based upon doctrine but the practice of Matthew 5:23, 24 (KJV): 'Therefore if thou bring thy gift to the altar, and there rememberest that thy brother hath ought against thee; Leave there thy gift before the altar, and go thy way; first be reconciled to thy brother, and then come and offer thy gift.' Discipleship is based upon Matthew 5:39: 'But I say unto you, That ye resist not evil: but whosoever shall smite thee on thy right cheek, turn to him the other also'.

We can 'if' and 'but' and 'um' and 'aagh' as to what Jesus meant here but it is quite clear, we should not repay evil for evil, even if we are labelled a 'wimp' for walking away from a fight. True discipleship is based upon Matthew 5:44, 'Love your enemies, bless them that curse you, do good to them that hate you, and pray for them which despitefully use you, and persecute you'.

True discipleship in the manifesto of God is based upon forgiving a brother or sister who sins against us irrespective of the amount of times they sin against us and irrespective of the severity in which we have been sinned against (Matthew 18:21, 22). True discipleship means we refuse to entertain or join in gossip concerning our brothers or sisters, the manifesto states that we must control this unruly member (James 3:9-12), the tongue. True discipleship is not simply about knowing or teaching doctrine, it is about living a life based upon the presence of the Holy Spirit in our body temple.

God's promises are then compared to the promises and claims of politicians. The pastor emphasises the security of God's promises and the relative magnificence of our contributions to the contract with God. The minister closes the sermon with an 'appeal' to the members of the congregation to believe in God's promises and to live in the light of their relationship to God.

The claims of the manifesto The manifestoes of the Conservatives, Labour and Liberal Democrats all make bold claims as to how they will change the country for the better if elected. The problem is, however, come Friday April 10, the elected government may ignore some of their promises or be powerless to fulfil them... not so with Jesus! In his manifesto, Jesus promised us rent and mortgage free housing in his Father's Kingdom (John 14:1-3). In the manifesto, Jesus promised that the bodies which we now have which are ravaged by disease and death will be exchanged for immortal bodies (1 Corinthians 15: 50-57). In the manifesto, Jesus promises that in the United Kingdom of God there will be no allocation of land for cemeteries for there will be no death in His Kingdom (1 Corinthians 15:55). In the manifesto, Jesus promises that there will be no hospitals, doctors, nurses, pills, medicines. He promises that there will be no AIDS, cancer, sickle cell, bad back or rheumatism, no arthritis or any manner of disease or sickness (Revelation 22:1-3). Jesus in the manifesto promises that there will be no Kleenex tissues, for no one will shed a tear in sorrow (Revelation 21:4). Jesus in his manifesto promises the absence of fear and terror, all nature will be brought into perfect harmony. The wolf will lie down in peace beside the lamb, a little child will not fear the lion nor the parents be concerned over their safety (Isaiah 11: 6-9). Jesus promises to establish a city on earth which will be called the New Jerusalem. This city will have streets paved with pure gold. Only the finest materials will go into the construction of the city's buildings and walls (Revelation 21: 10-14).

What will it cost? But surely promises cost money. The Conservative party is accusing the Labour party of using figures which do not add up. The Conservatives say this country cannot afford Labour's spending proposals. Labour's spending proposals will result in much higher taxes for everyone, they claim. But, my friends, the promises of Jesus will cost us nothing, because it has already cost him everything when he shed his blood for us on Calvary. All that Jesus asks of us is to sur-

> render our life to Him. And, my friends, unlike the politicians of today, what Jesus promises, He delivers.
>
> **Appeal** The apostle Peter said 'be all the more eager to make your calling and election sure. For if you do these things, you will never fall, and you will receive a rich welcome into the eternal Kingdom of our Lord and Saviour Jesus Christ' (2 Peter 2: 10,11)
>
> Someone here today needs to make their calling and election sure. Someone here today needs to cast a vote for Jesus Christ and the manifesto of his Kingdom. Someone here today needs to give their life to the Lord. Someone here today needs to make a stand for Jesus Christ, to be baptised and follow His will. Who will vote for Jesus today?

This lengthy quote from a recent sermon illustrates how the 'faith factor' is central to the belief of such congregations. Faith provides members with the capacity to deal with oppressive forces, whether translated via racism or other forms of injustice, evil or sin.

Belief Systems and Oppression

Cohen and Taylor (1972) examined the role that belief systems play in enabling individuals to deal with long-term oppressive situations. In the exploration of the ways in which 'lifers' survive in prisons, Cohen and Taylor identified various methods of psychological survival. They noted how human behaviour can be understood with reference to people's belief systems.

> When we comment upon a particular individual's behaviour in everyday life we ascribe an ideology to him which serves as a casual string upon which to thread a variety of apparently unrelated actions (p.24).

Cohen and Taylor noted that these props are not so much internal ones derived from the personality, but more exterior strengths of a particular ideological loyalty. Religion was one such taken-for-granted 'prop' at times when people experience long fasts or extreme physical deprivation.

Thus Robin Knox-Johnston, the round-the-world boatsman, observed that 'throughout the voyage I never really felt I was completely alone, and I think a man would have to be inhumanly confident and self-reliant if he were to make this sort of voyage without belief in God'.

The use of religion as a sustaining ideology for people facing physical deprivation have been documented in other places. Cohen and Taylor show also how significant the protective and insulative nature of personal ideologies and convictions can be. They regard sustaining ideologies as crucial to survival in extreme situations.

> It seems that most prisoners tried to protect themselves against the initial shock by mustering forces helpful in supporting their badly shaken self-esteem. Those groups which found in their past life some basis for the erection of such a buttress to their endangered egos seemed to survive (p.84).

The church obviously continues to play a central role in the lives of many African-Caribbean British citizens. Social mobility or marrying across a racial divide has not necessarily rendered the values and community spirit irrelevant to their lives.

In a final attempt to question the possible overstatement of the positive or functional role of the church, I conclude by presenting the current experiences of black British citizens in another welfare institution. The study focused its attention on the impact religion has had in the educational experiences of black people. By looking at the experiences of black people in another institution, we are left questioning the extent to which religious adherence or affiliation can counteract the racist oppression which is endemic in British society.

Welfare organisations and black communities

The previous chapters have clearly identified the negative experiences of black children in British schools. To contextualise this experience adequately in what is, after all, a welfare organisation, it seemed valuable to examine black people's experiences in at least one other welfare organisation. Could it be that teachers, as professionals in one setting, operate differently to other white professionals in other settings, for example, Social Services Departments? While institutional and individual racism was shown as endemic in British schools the assumption that it exists in other settings needs to be tested. Many of the respondents recalled white individuals, teachers, college lecturers, employers whose personal interest proved invaluable in the subject's educational progress (see Chapters four and five). Many white social workers have declared their personal and professional, individual and group commitment to generally anti-oppressive and specificly anti-racist social work practice (Channer and Parton, 1990). Notions of 'rainbow coalitions', the working together of oppressed groups, have been offered as legitimate options for opposing racism. There are, however, black community members and practitioners who see same-race client-worker relationships, indeed separate services for black clients, as the only meaningful way forward. They are often suspicious of declarations of goodwill and subscribe to CLR James's (1938) view that: 'The black will know as friends only those whites who are fighting in the ranks beside them'.

A brief but comprehensive examination of the current role of the personal social services in the lives of black people may provide us with a wider framework from which we can assess the experiences of black people in Britain. The negative impact of school experiences has caused many black individuals to fail to realise their career potential. Some (Small, 1989) argue that the consequences for black individuals and their communities have been severe but are at times retrievable. However the failings, malpractice and ill-informed interventions of individual practitioners working for social service departments have resulted in the undertaking, or cementing of criminal careers, and the onset or institutionalising of mental illness and death of black clients. If we are to test out the views expressed elsewhere in the study, we need to examine whether the black British experience of anomie, isolation and racism will almost inevitably end in further oppression at the hands of welfare professionals.

Liberal governments from 1905-1915 laid the foundations of the British Welfare State by introducing social services outside the Poor Law to help those in need. The Beveridge Report (1941) and major advances by the 1945-1951 Labour governments set in motion the concept of welfare resources based on need. Services grouped under the term Personal Social Service developed, aiming to promote the welfare of different groups of people with special needs. Many of these services made use of social work skills to offer separate and distinct statutory provision.

In the last twenty years there has been a growing awareness that black clients have been over-represented in the 'controlling aspect' of the personal social services, and particularly in mental health and taking children into care. But they are grossly under-represented in 'welfare aspects' of social work such as advice, guidance, counselling and respite care for elderly people. This position is almost inevitable given that much of the debate about social work with black families has been rooted in constructs of social pathology (Coombe and Little, 1986, Ahmed, Cheetham and Small, 1986). A Eurocentric framework is the basis on which many pathological assumptions are built. This deficit model has entered social work practice as the conventional wisdom that guides how black families are perceived and 'understood'. It determines the ways in which many white social workers view black people in general and shapes the style of social work carried out with black families. Small (1989) states that:

> The deficit model of the black family can cause further disruption or even exacerbate the difficulties caused by racism. This may well explain how a significant number of black family members become casualties of the system and are relegated to mental institutions, the prisons, children's homes, or fostering and adoption arrangements (pp.299-280)

The over representation of black children in 'care' demonstrates the severity of negative impact on the lives of black people. The 1960s and 1970s saw a rapid increase in the number of black children received into 'care'. Coombe (1986) described the process as looking as though driven by religious zeal. The number of black children being admitted to special schools during this period matched the number of black children being received into 'care'. The tendency for white professionals to receive black children from 'unstable families' (Fitzherbert, 1967) and assimilate them into white homes was widespread. This racist policy was covert, unlike the Australian government's policy on Aborigine children. However, throughout the education and training for social work and its practice, few challenged this 'raping' of black communities. Black professionals and community members expressed their strength of feeling when they stated that: 'White workers were encouraging a subtle form of slavery but this time only using black children' (Ely and Denny, 1987), p.91).

In terms of social work intervention, the apparent inversion of the tendency to 'rescue and assimilate' is the 'tendency to neutralise and ignore' (Channer and Parton, 1990). While black families may be subject to inappropriate and heavy-handed interventions, public inquiries and research suggest in child care cases that the opposite may also be increasingly happening. The problem appears to be the failure of practitioners to identify high-risk structures and thereby failing to protect children. This failure is seen to be crucially associated with a pervasive optimism among social workers which is in part a result of their cultural relativist stance in assessing black families (see Channer and Parton, 1990, p.111).

Social workers and their managers are deemed to be substitute parents for children who have been admitted to their care. However there is little evidence that these 'substitute parents' always act in the best interest of black children. In the 1989 Children Act, the concept of partnership has been formally established in statute. Previously, a philosophy of partnership and accountability was deemed to be good social work practice. Marsh *et.al.* (1986) outlined their understanding of partnership in public child care services as:

> ... a philosophy of practice which could inform all the actions undertaken by social workers, so that clients could reasonably ask for an account to be given, and expect their views to carry weight in connection with the child care processes they are experiencing (p.140).

In practice, however, this idealised vision of accountable, receptive, responsive workers was not the regular experience of black clients. The death of Jasmine Beckford (1984) and Tyra Henry (1986), two black children in the 'care' of social workers, again provoked anxiety about the quality of social work intervention for black clients.

Given the grave dissatisfaction registered by black individuals and groups about the mainstream services they have been offered, it is not surprising that there is a groundswell of opinion in black communities advocating for separate services. A growing number of black voluntary projects have emerged in response to the failure of social services departments to provide satisfactory welfare services for black communities. Many of these self-help projects have been set up by community organisations such as churches. To date, the largest proportion has focused on the needs of black elders. Black voluntary projects range from luncheon and social clubs and day centres to sheltered housing developments. Elders are provided with lunches, either prepared by themselves on the premises or supplied by appropriate restaurants or specialist bulk suppliers. Many such clubs provide not only meals but a convenient place for informal meetings, as well as some social activities. Some projects also take meals to the housebound or provide transport to the centre, where they can mix with other elders rather than eat alone at home. Various religious and cultural organisations have undertaken the task of providing the missing information and knowledge of welfare rights and services. Advice and counselling services are integrated in these self-help projects. Lallje comments that:

> Black self help organisations have, with minimal funding if at all, provided facilities which black elders feel to be fitting, where they can feel comfortable and where facilities have been geared to their needs. It is the existence of such facilities that have rendered black elders visible: without them, these elders would have remained scattered and invisible (Quoted in Glendenning and Pearson, 1988, p.55).

'Tender Touch' was advertised in November 1991, as a small children's home based in Catford South East London, which caters for children and young people aged between 7 and 17 years. 'Tender Touch' is unusual in that it caters primarily for black children. Unlike larger residential units, this home claims to provide children with a warm and safe family setting based in a multiracial community. The staff group are predominantly African-Caribbean.

Despite their best intentions these self-help projects cannot adequately reach all sections of the black communities or provide a comprehensive range of services. Most self-help projects rely on temporary sources of funding, including inner city and urban programme funds. Section 11 of the 1966 Act, and Training Council Commission (formerly the MSC) grants fund the staff salaries of many of these projects. Not only are the funds temporary (and short-term) but there are usually several funding agencies involved, including partnerships with local authorities and voluntary organisations, as well as the personal contributions of community members.

Problems of staff shortages are exacerbated by the lack of future funds on a regular basis. Attracting funds is a consuming activity. Many organisers and project co-ordinators lose their way in the plethora of information, or falter in the absence of 'know-how' of the complex funding system. So many projects struggle to survive rather than being able to expand and offer the service needed.

Many would therefore argue that the need to set up such separate and specialised services justifies the claims that black people have a marginal existence in British society. As black people are part of society, they are entitled to mainstream services and should be offered adequate and culturally appropriate services.

It could be argued that self-help projects and other black voluntary initiatives offer an alternative to statutory provision. However Patel (1990) points out that an alternative implies a choice in the matter and allows free entry into the statutory sector. But various forces, eg racism in its many forms, or linguistic difficulties, act as barriers against the potential use of statutory services by black clients. Social services departments, like other welfare organisations, view black communities as marginal to mainstream provision. They therefore find it convenient to support self-help projects, because these act as a 'buffer' against direct criticism of social services departments for failing to provide adequate mainstream provision. These projects act as the 'interface' between the social service departments and a potential black political uprising by black community members for their civil rights.

To advocate separate welfare services for black communities could, ironically, prove disadvantageous to the communities. However, acknowledging the individual and group initiatives in black communities helps to temper the prevailing image of black individuals as victims. The collective strength and resourcefulness and insightful planning shown by black groups registers the need for social workers and their organisations to move away from pathological assumptions and deficient models which have become conventional social work wisdom.

In Chapter four and five and elsewhere in this book, the commitment of white individuals to antiracism has been noted. It is therefore misleading to suggest that all white practitioners are overt or even covert racists. However, in their attempt to understand and work with what seems to them to be a predominance of deviant behaviour in black communities and black families, white professionals may move away from notions of pathological personalities. Instead they may regard the 'obvious' endemic deviant behaviour in black communities as a result of the culture and the structure of society itself.

Merton (1968) offers analysis of social structure and deviance which suggests that deviant behaviour from certain communities may be inevitable. Interestingly, Mertonian theory is often offered on social work courses as underpinning social theory that presents a range of theoretical perspectives. However, on closer observation, it appears that this contribution to social work education and training is likely to confirm a pathological view. Merton begins from the standard functionalist position of value consensus, suggesting that all members of society share the same values. Moreover, since members of society are differently positioned in the social structure they may differ in terms of, for example, class position, so do not have the same opportunity of realising the shared values. This situation, he suggests, can generate deviance. He asserts that:

> The social and cultural structure generates pressure for social deviant behaviour upon people variously located in that structure (1986, p.24).

Merton outlines five possible ways in which members of society can respond to achieving success goals. He regards 'conformity' as the most common response. Members of society conform to both success goals and the normative means of reaching them. They strive for success by means of accepted channels. A second response is 'innovation', which he defines as rejecting normative means of achieving success for deviant means, in particular, crime. Merton argues that members of the lower social strata are most likely to select this route to success as they are least likely to succeed through conventional channels. So there is greater pressure on them to deviate. Their educational qualifications are usually low, their jobs provide little opportunity for advancement. Innovation is seen as an alternative route to the conventional and legitimate channels, which appear to be blocked. Lower middle class individuals are regarded as prime targets for the third of Merton's responses: 'ritualism'. Unlike the working class, these individuals have been strongly socialised to conform to social norms, so are restrained from turning to crime. Instead they scale down or abandon their success goals. 'Retreatism' — the fourth option — is not related to social class. It is used by those who have strongly internalised both the cultural goals and the conventional means, yet they are unable to achieve success. These people became unable to cope with the resulting tension and therefore 'drop out' of society, defeated and resigned to their failure. Lastly, he regards 'rebellion' as:

> a rejection of both success goals and institutionalised means and their replacement by different goals and means' (Haralambos, 1980, p.415).

Interactionist theories of human behaviour challenge the deterministic bias of such structural theories of deviance. And Merton himself softens the suggestion that the boundaries between these responses are rigidly defined and says that some degree of overlap may occur between categories. My major concern with Merton's selection of categories is that he appears to omit even the possibility of members of the lower classes finding an individual or collective form of resistance which they could use as a 'buffer' against obvious social pressures to behave deviantly. If differently framed, the categories of 'innovation' or 'rebellion' can well encompass notions of positive resistance. Social work practitioners and other professionals, who regard members of black communities as inevitable victims, oppressed by endemic and pervasive racism, ignore or neglect the resourceful, purposeful insights and initiatives generated by individuals and groups within these communities. Social work, perhaps more than other welfare institution, promotes the centrality of client self-determination in professional practice. Although referring to social science research, Matza's (1969) message (see Chapter one) is equally applicable to social work practice. He reminds researchers that:

> A serious commitment to the subjective view cannot grudgingly stop with the appreciation of the subject's definition of his specific deviant predicament. It must also entail an appreciation of the ordinary subject's philosophical definition of this general predicament. Concretely, this means that the capacity to intend must be treated seriously and occupy a central place in the analysis on social life (p.25).

The respondents' own views about how they progress despite oppressive forces has been central to this study. I understand their 'capacity for intent' to mean the element of resourcefulness that can take them beyond their obvious difficulties. The exploration of this apparent resourcefulness has focused on black people's educational experiences. Could it be that the attempt to project this individual and community capacity to resist the racism in the personal social services is too idealistic? The individual and group initiatives within black communities, described in this chapter, clearly demonstrate the capacity to redeem a position of neglect by mainstream social service departments. However, the continuing over-representation of black people in the 'controlling' aspects of the personal social services is disturbing. The Institute of Race Relations (1991) gives accounts of the ill treatment and eventual deaths of black people at the hands of the police. Social workers and probation officers often find it necessary to seek the 'support' of the police when engaged with the controlling aspects of social work practice. Police assistance with the compulsory admission to hospital of the mentally ill is common practice. In *Deadly Silence* (1991) the Institute for Race Relations report that over 58 black individuals died while in the custody of the police, or in a special hospital. In many of these cases the mental condition of the prisoners was a significant issue. The close link between social workers and the police is highlighted in the 'Roll-call of death' — a chilling account of the circumstances surrounding these deaths. Edwin Robinson aged 28, hanged himself in Brixton prison, for example. He had been diagnosed as suffering from a psychotic illness, but social workers did not appear in court so that he could not be sent to hospital under Section 2 of the Mental Health Act. The coroner made several recommendations about the urgent need for better communication between courts, prisons and allied professionals.

Could it be that however resilient the black community and whatever capacity to resist oppressive forces elements within certain welfare organisations are too pervasive, endemic and overwhelming to counteract? The Institute of Race Relations (1991) observes that:

> Too many of us have died without cause, since first we came to work for this country in the post war years... Or if cause there be,.. it is the racist bias that has been woven into, and become an extricable part of, the culture and administration of these 'services'.
>
> The contempt for blacks on the streets is carried into the contempt for blacks in their homes, for black family life. The black man's home is not his castle, even less the black woman's hers. There is nothing inviolable about the black family... Racial diagnosis, it would appear, over-rides clinical diagnosis. Thus young African-Caribbeans who exhibit what is considered odd or anti-social behaviour are commonly diagnosed as schizophrenic... Little attempt is made to seek the cause

> of the 'patient's' behaviour in his (and invariably it's a he) particular history or the anomie visited on him by a racist society' (pp.1-2).

While reading *Deadly Silence* I realised that a number of the deceased had been members of the very churches and sects discussed in the study. This realisation seemed to call into question much of the arguments advanced in this book. The idea that the theological messages, community support and other aspects of church affiliation provides black Christians with a 'buffer against racism' might evidently not be universally applicable.

I have sought to indicate the coping strategies utilised by black British people. By highlighting the sustaining ideologies adopted by black people the work has generated a discussion about the functions education and religion might have for black people in oppressive systems. Bell hooks (1989) examines the potential role of education thus:

> Education either functions as an instrument which is used to facilitate the integration of the younger generation into the logic of the present system and bring out conformity to it, or it becomes 'the practice of freedom', the means by which the men and women deal critically and creatively with reality and discover how to participate in the transformation of the world.

Black people have struggled against racist oppression to obtain a reasonable standard of education. They have recognised its worth in accessing some of society's resources. Some black people have noted the ways in which religion and education have been used to oppress and reinforce systems of domination. However, for many black people, like the life history subjects in this study, religion and education can be viewed as channels for freedom. Both provide a psychological and social framework within which black people can operate effectively in a racist society.

Bibliography

Abelson, N. R. (1977) *Person; A Study of Philosophical Psychology.* London: MacMillan

Ahmed, S. Cheetham and Small J. (eds) (1986) *Social work with black children and their families.* London: Batsford

Akbar, N. (1984) *Chain and Image of Psychological Slavery.* New Jersey: New Mind Productions

Alibhai-Brown, Y. and Montague, A. (1992) *The Colour of Love.* London: Virago Press

Allport, G. (1942) *The Use of Personal Document in Psychological Science.* New York: Social Science Research Council

ALTARF (1984) *Challenging Racism.* London: ALTARF

Aspinwall, K. (1985) A biographical approach to the professional development of teachers. MEd no. 375 Sheffield University

Ball, S. and Goodson, I. (eds) (1985) *Teachers' lives and careers.* Lewes: Falmer Press

Bagley, C., Bart, M., Wong, J. (1978) 'Cognition and Scholastic success in West Indian 10-year-olds in London: a comparative study' *Educational Studies*, Vol. 4 No. 1 pp.7-17

Bagley, C. Verma G. (1979) *Race, Education and Identity.* London: MacMillan

Barnes, D. (1986) *Language, the Learner and the School.* Harmondsworth: Penguin

Barratt, L. E. (1971) *The Rastafarians.* London: Heinemann

Becker, H. S. (1986) *Writing for Social Scientists.* Chicago Press.

Becker, H. S. (1952) 'Social class variations in the teacher-pupil relationship' *Journal of Educational Psychology* in M. Keddie (1971) 'Classroom Knowledge' in M. F. D. Young (ed) Knowledge and Control p.125 London, Routledge and Kegan Paul

Becker, H. (1963) 'Outsiders'. *Studies in Sociology of Deviance.* New York: Free Press bell hooks (1989) *Talking black thinking feminist thinking black,* Boston: Sheba Feminist Publications

Bell, J. et al (1984) *Conducting small scale investigations in educational management.* Milton Keynes: Harper Education Series with Oxford University Press

Berger, P. (1976) *A Sociological View of Religion.* London: Faber and Faber

Bernard, V (1983) Is the church the radical alternative. unpublished Masters Thesis. South London Polytechnic

Bhatnager, J. (1970) *Immigrants at School.* London: Cornmarket Press

Blumer, H. (1939) *Critiques of Research in the Social Sciences: An Appraisal of Thomas and Znaniecki's 'The Polish Peasant in Europe and America'*. New York: Social Science Research Council

Blyth, E. and Milner, J. (1988) Schools and Pupils' Families (unpublished)

Bogardus, E. S. (1933) 'A social distance scale'. *Sociology and Social Research* 34, 5, pp.365-373

Brandt, G. (1984) British Youth Caribbean Creole — The Politics of Resistance. Paper presented at the conference on Languages. Thames Polytechnic 31 August — 3 September 1984

Brienburg, P. (1986) 'Language Attitudes: The Case of Caribbean Languages' in *The Language of the Black Experience*, Sutcliffe (ed). Oxford: Basil Blackwell

Breinburg, P. (1984b) 'Cultural Racism and Books'. *Dragon's Teeth* 19

Brienburg, P. (1984c) Exploring Future in Language and Education, a comparative study. Unpublished PhD thesis submitted to Keele University

Brittan, E. (1976) 'Multiracial Education, Teachers' Opinions on Aspects of School Life, Pupils and Teachers', *Educational Research* Vol. 18 No. 3

Brock, C. (ed) (1986) *The Caribbeans in Europe.* Gainsborough: Frank Cass

Brothers, J. (1964) *Religious Institutions.* London: Longman

Brown, M. (1986) 'The New Middle Class' in *Woman's Journal,* October, pp.112-116

Bryan, B. Dadzie, S. Scape, S. (1985), *The Heart of the Race: black women's lives in Britain.* London: Virago

Bulmer, M. (1984) *The Chicago School of Sociology.* Chicago University Press

Bultler, S. and Wintram, C. (1991) *Feminist Groupwork.* London: Sage

Burgess, E. W. (1927) 'Statistics and case studies as methods of sociological research'. *Sociology and Social Research* 12, pp.103-120

Burgess, G. (1982) *Field Research: A Source Book and Field Manual.* Allen and Unwin

Calley, M. J. (1965) *God's People — West Indian Pentecostalist Sects in England.* Oxford University Press

Carey, J. T. (1975) *Sociology and Public Affairs.* The Chicago School: Sage

Cashmore, E. (1979) *Rastaman.* London: Allen and Unwin

Cashmore, E. (1982) *Black Sportsmen.* London: Routledge and Kegan Paul

Cashmore, E. (1984) *No Future: Youth and Society.* Heinemann

Cashmore, E. (1984) *Dictionary of race and ethnicity.* London: Routledge and Kegan Paul

Channer, Y. and Channer V. Y. 'African Caribbean Christian First Generation Women'. International Women's Day Conference at Sheffield City Polytechnic (taped conversations)

Channer, Y. (1978) A study of the problems faced by West Indian children in British schools (unpublished)

Channer, Y. and Parton, N. (1990) 'Racism, cultural relativism and child protection' in The Violence against Children Study Group (ed) *Taking Child Abuse Seriously.* London: Unwin Hyman Ltd

Chevannes, M. (1982) Interview on 'Ebony' London BBC

Chigwada, R. (1987) 'Not victims not superwomen', *Spare Rib.* No. 183, pp.14-18

Clark, F. Ferguson (1978) *The Religious Perspective: African Religions.* Milton Keynes: Open University Press

Clarke, A. M. and Clarke A. D. B. (1976) *Early Experience in Myth and Evidence.* London: Open Books

Clarke, E. (1957) *My Mother Who Fathered Me.* London: Allen and Unwin

Cleage, A. B. Jr (1978) *Black Christian Nation — New directions for the black church.* New York: Free Press

Coard, B. (1971) *How the West Indian Child is Made Educationally Subnormal in the British School System.* London: New Beacon Books

Cohen, S. and Taylor, L. (1972) *Psychological Survival.* Harmondsworth: Penguin

Community Relations Commission (1974) *Educational Needs and Children from Minority Groups.* London: CRE

Cone, J. H. (1969) *Black Theology and Black Power.* New York: The Seabury Press

Cone, J. H. (1975) *God of the Oppressed.* New York: The Seabury Press Inc

Cone, J. H. (1986) *My Soul Looks Back.* New York: Orbis Books

Cone, J. H., (1990) *A Black Theology of Liberation.* New York: Orbis Books

Cross, M. (1987) 'The Black Economy', *New Society* Vol. 81 No. 1282 pp.16-18 24 July

Cross, M. (1987) 'A cause for concern: ethnic minority youth and vocational training policy'. Policy Paper No. 8 Centre for Research in Ethnic Relations. Warwick

Cruse, H. (1967). *The Crises of the Negro Intellectual.* New York: William Marrow

Crystal, D. (1974) *What is Linguistics?* London: Edward Arnold

Dalphinis, M. (1985) *Caribbean and African Language: Social History, Language, Literature and Education.* London: Karia Press

Dalton, H. (1989) 'Aids in Blackface', *Journal of the American Academy of Arts and Science* Vol. II No. 3 pp.87-103

Denzin, N. K. (1970) *The Research Act in Sociology.* Chicago: Aldine

Denzin, N. K. (1971) *Childhood and Socialisation.* London: Jossey-Bass Publishers

Denzin, N. K. (1989) *Interpretive Interactionism.* London: Sage

Denzin, N. K. (1989) *Interpretative Biography.* Vol. 17. London: Sage

Dodgson, E. (1984) *Motherland.* London: Heinemann Educational Books

Drew, D. and Gray, J. (1989) 'The fifth year examination achievements of Black young people in England and Wales'. Unpublished paper. University of Sheffield Educational Research Centre

Driver, G. (1980) *Beyond Underachievement: Case studies in English, West Indian and Asian school leavers at sixteen plus.* London: Commission for Racial Equality

Driver, G. (1977) 'Cultural competence, social power and school achievement: West Indian secondary school pupils in the West Midlands. *New Community.* Vol. 5 No. 4 pp.353-9

Durkheim, E. (1947) *The Division of Labour.* New York: The Free Press

Edwards, V. (1979) *The West Indian Language Issue in British schools:. Challenges and responses.* London: Routledge and Kegan Paul

Eggleston, J, (1985), 'The educational and vocational experience of young black Britons', *Multicultural Teaching* Vol 4 No 1

Elmer, T. Clark (1937) *The Small Sects in America.* Nashville: Cooksburg Press

Essen, J. and Ghodsian, M. (1979) 'The Children of Immigrants: School Performances' in *New Community* Vol. 7 No. 3 pp.422-9

Essen-Valan, E. (1966) *Black nationalism. The Race of Black Muslims in USA.* Harmondsworth: Penguin

Ely, P. and Denny, O. (1987) *Social Work in a Multiracial Society.* London: Gower

Evetts, J, (1989), Married Women and Careers: Career history accounts of primary head teachers. *Qualitative Studies in Education 1989* Vol. 2, No. 2, pp 89-105

Eysenk, H. J. (1971) *Race, Intelligence and Education.* London: Temple Smith

Fanon, F. (1952) *Black Skin, White Mask.* London: Pluto Press

Fanon, F. (1965) *A Dying Colonation.* Earthscan

Fanon, F. (1967) *Wretched of the Earth.* Harmondsworth: Penguin

Farraday, A. and Plummer, K. (1979) 'Doing Life Histories'. *Sociological Review* Vol. 27, No. 4, pp.773-798

Fay, B. (1975) *Social Theory and Political Practice.* London: Allen and Unwin

Ferguson, J. (1984) 'The Laboratory of Racism'. *New Scientist* pp.11-20. 27 September

Fielding, N. G. and Fielding, J. L. (1986) *Linking Data.* London: Sage

Fitzherbert, K. (1967), *West Indian Children in London.* London: J Bell and Sons

Fuller, M. (1980) 'Black girls in a London comprehensive school' reprinted in M Hammersley and P Woods (eds) 1984. *Life is School.* Milton Keynes: Open University Press.

Frankenberg, R. (1963) 'Participant observers'. *New Society*, Vol. 1, No. 23, pp.22-3

Fryer, P. (1984) *Staying Power: the history of black people in Britain.* London: Pluto Press

Furlong, V. J. (1985) *The Deviant Pupil: Sociological Perspectives.* Milton Keynes: Open University

Gibson, A. and Barrow, J. (1986) *The Unequal Struggle.* London: The Centre for Caribbean Studies

Gidden, A. (1976) *New Rules of Sociological Methods: A positive critique of interpretative sociologies.* London: Hutchinson

Giles, R. *The West Indian Experience in British schools: multiracial education in London.* London: Heinemann

Gillborn, D. (1990) *Race, Ethnicity and Education.* London: Unwin Hyman

Gilroy, P. (1987) *There ain't no black in the 'Union Jack': the cultural politics of 'race' and nation.* London: Hutchinson

Glaser, B. G. and Strauss, A. L. (1967) *The Discovery of Grounded Theory.* Chicago: Aldine

Glendenning, F. and Pearson, M. (1988) *The Black and Ethnic Minority Elders in Britain, health needs and access to services.* Working Papers on the Health of Older People No. 6, Health Education Authority and Keele University

Goode, E. (1967) 'Some Critical Observations of the Church Sect Dimension — Church Sects Reappraised'. *Journal for the Scientific Study of Religion* 6(1) 69-76

Goffman, E. (1968) *Asylum.* Harmondsworth: Penguin

Goodson, I. F. (1992) *Studying Teacher's Lives.* London: Routledge

Griffiths, K. (1982) 'British, West Indian and Asian Children — Assessing Conceptual Development'. *New Community* 9, 3 pp.407-22

Grumet, M. (1981) 'Restitution and reconstruction of education experience: an autobiographical method for curriculum theory' in Lawn, M. and Barton, L. (eds) *Rethinking Curriculum Studies* pp.115-130. London: Croom Helm

Hall, S. (1989) 'Race, articulation and societies structured in dominance' *Sociological Theories: Race and Colonialism.* UNESCO

Hammersley, M. (1989) *The Dilemma of Qualitative Method. Herbert Blumer and the Chicago Tradition.* London: Routledge

Handel, W. (1982) *Ethnomethdology. How people make sense.* New Jersey: Prentice-Hall

Haralambos, M. (1985) *Sociology Themes and Perspectives.* London: Bell and Hyman

Hernton, C. (1969) *Sex and Racism.* London: Granada

Hewitt, R. (1986) *White Talk, Black Talk.* Cambridge: Cambridge University Press

Hick, J. (1963) *Philosophy of Religion.* New Jersey: Prentice-Hall

Hick, J. (1979) *Christianity and Race in Britain Today.* Birmingham: AFFOR

Hick, J. (1988) *Faith and Knowledge.* London: MacMillan Press Ltd

Hill, C. (1970) 'Some Aspects of Race and Religion in Britain' in *A Sociological Yearbook of Religion in Britain*, pp.30-44

Hill, C. (1971) 'Pentecostalist growth — result of racialism?' *Race Today* Vol. 3 pp.187-190

Hincliffe, M. (1985) Two special needs teachers their lives; an interactive analysis of significant life events and their relationship to teacher style. MEd no. 393, University of Sheffield

Hollenweger, W. (1974) *Pentecost between Black and White.* Belfast: Christian Journals Ltd

Houghton, V. P. (1966) *A Report on the Scores of West Indian Immigrant Children and English Children on an Individually Administered Test.* London: Institute of Race Relations

Husband, C. (ed) (1982) *Race and British Society. E354 Ethnic Minorities and Community Relations Units 5-7.* Milton Keynes: Open University

Institute of Race Relations (1991) *Deadly Silence — Black Deaths in Custody.* London: Institute of Race Relations

James CLR (1980) *Spheres of Existence: Selecting Writings.* London: Alison and Busby

Jamdaigni, L., Phillips-Bell, M. and Ward, J. (1982) *Talking Chalk.* Birmingham: AFFOR

Jeffcoate, R. (1979) *Positive Image: Towards a multiracial curriculum.* London: Chameleon Press

Jenkins, R. (1966) Address given by the Home Secretary to a Meeting of Voluntary Liason Committees

Jenson, A. R. (1969) 'How much can we boost IQ and scholastic achievement?' *Harvard Educational Review,* Vol. 39, No. 1, pp.1-123

Johns, G. (1986) 'Black Parents' Movement'. *Report of a Conference on Education and Young Black People*, 10 May. Organised by Trade Union and Basic Education Project in conjunction with Manchester City Council Education Committee

Jones, V. A. (1986) *We are our own educators.* London: Karia Press

Jones, W. A. (1979) *God in the Ghetto.* Newark: Progressive Baptist Publishing House

Kerr, L. (1991) The Afro-Caribbean Family in Britain: Scriptural Authoritarianism and a New Testament Alternative. Unpublished thesis. MPhil University of Birmingham

King Jnr, M. L. (1963) *Strength to Love.* London: Fount Paperbacks

Kitsuse, J. I. and Cicourel, A. V. (1963) 'A note on the Uses of Official Statistics'. *Social Problem*, 11, Fall, pp.131-139

Klockars, C. B. (1974) *The Professional Fence.* New York: Free Press

Labov, W. (1972) 'The Logic of non-standard English', in Giglioli, P. P. (ed) *Language and Social Context.* Harmondsworth, Penguin. pp.179-215

Langan, M. and Lee, P. (eds) (1989) *Radical Social Work Today.* London: Unwin Hyman

Lashley, H. (1980) 'The new black magic', *British Journal of Physical Education* Vol. 11 No. 1 pp.5-6 January

Lashley, H. (1986) Prospects and Problems of the Afro-Caribbeans in the British Education System in Brock, C. (ed) *The Caribbean in Europe.* Gainsborough: Frank Cass

Lawrence, E. (1981) 'White sociology, black struggle'. *Multiracial Education* 9(3) pp.43-48

Lewis, D. L. (1970) *Martin Luther King, Jr.* Harmondsworth: Penguin

Lincoln, L. E. (1961) *The Black Muslims in America.* Boston: Beacon Press

Linoski, G. (1963) *The religious factor: a sociological enquiry.* New York: Doubleday

Little, A. (1975) 'The Educational Achievement of Ethnic Minority Children in London Schools' in Verma, G. K. and Bagley, C. (eds) *Race and Education Across Cultures.* London: Heinemann

Liverpool, V. (1986) 'When backgrounds clash: Understanding cultural norms among non-white clients'. *Community Care,* 2 October pp. 119-21

McEwan, E. C., Gipps, C. V. and Sumner, R. (1975) *Language Proficiency in the Multi-racial Junior School.* Slough: NFER

McClelland, D. C. (1961) *The achieving society.* London: Van Nostrand

Mabey, C. (1986) 'Black pupils' achievements in Inner London'. *Educational Research* Vol. 28 No. 3rd November, pp.163-173

Mac an Ghaill, M. (1988) *Young Gifted and Black: Student-Teacher Relations in the Schooling of Black Youth.* Milton Keynes: Open University Press

Mac an Ghaill, M. (1989) 'Beyond the white norm: the use of qualitative methods in the study of black youths' schooling in England'. *Qualitative Studies in Education* Vol. 2 No. 3 pp.175-189

Mackintosh, N. J. and Mascie-Taylor, C. G. (1985) 'The IQ Question' in DES: *Education for All*: The Report of the committee of Inquiry into the Education of Children from Ethnic Minority Groups (The Swann Report). HMSO

Malcolm X (1970) *Afro American History.* New York: Pathfinder

Malinowski, B. (1922) *Argonauts of the Western Pacific.* London: Routledge and Kegan Paul

Mangham, I. L. (1986) *Power and Performance in Organization: An exploration of executive process.* Oxford: Blackwell

Majoribanks, K. (1980) *Ethnic Families and Children's Achievement.* London: Allen and Unwin

Marsh et al. (1986) *In and Out of Care.* London: Batsford and BAAF

Martin, D. A. (1962) 'The Denomination'. *British Journal of Sociology* 13, 1, pp.1-14

Martin, D. (1967) *A Sociology of English Religions.* London: Heinemann

Matza, D. (1969) *Becoming Deviant.* New Jersey: Prentice Hall

Mazrui A. A. (1986) *The Africans: A Triple Heritage.* London: BBC

Megenn, R. J. (1979) Peer networks and school performance. Unpublished PhD dissertation. University of Aston: Birmingham

Meikle, J. (1991) 'Afro-Caribbean students more likely to drop degree courses than whites and Asians, study claims'. *The Guardian*, 14 Jan, p.23

Merton, R.K. (1968) *Social Theory and Social Structures*. New York: The Free Press

Mbiti, J. S. (1969) *African religions and philosophy*. London: Heinemann

Middleton, B. (1983) Factors affecting the performance of West Indian boys in a secondary School. Unpublished MA dissertation, University of York

Milner, D. (1975) *Children and Race*. Harmondsworth: Penguin

Milroy, J. L. (1985) *Authority in Language*.' London: Routledge and Kegan Paul

Milroy, L. (1980) *Language and Social Networks*. Oxford Blackwell

Milroy, L. (1987) *Observing and Analysing Natural Language*. Oxford: Basil Blackwell

Miranda, J. P. (1979) *Marx and the Bible*. New York: Orbis Books

Mobery, D. A. (1964) *The Church as a Social Institution*. New Jersey: Prentice-Hall

Modood, T. (1988) 'Who's defining who?' *New Society*, 4th March, p.4-5

Moore, R. (1966) 'Religion in Society in the urban twilight zone'. *The Listener*, May 26 pp.753-755

National Youth Bureau (1987) 'Young blacks face bias on YTS' in *The Teacher* p.4 12 January

Neibuhr, R. H. (1929) *The Social Sources of Denominationalism*. New York: Free Press

Nelson, V. (1985) *Writers' Block and How to Use it*. Cincinnati, Ohio: Writers Digest Books

Niles, N. A. and Gardener, T. G. (eds) (1978) *Perspectives in West Indian Education*. Michigan: Michigan State University

Nyerere, J. (1974) *Man and Development*. Oxford: Oxford University Press

Onyeama, D. (1977) *Nigger at Eton*. London: Satellite Books

Palmer, F. (ed) (1986) *Antiracism: an Assault on Education and Values*. London: Sherwood

Park, R. (1937) in Stonequist, E. *The Marginal Man*. New York: Scribners

Parlett, M. and Hamilton, I. (1972) 'Evaluation and Illumination: a new approach to the study of innovatory programmes'. *Centre for Research in the Educational Sciences, University of Edinburgh Occasional Paper 9*

Parris, J. and Hale, M. (1983) *Achievement and Inequality in Education. A Reader for Conflict and Change in Education. A sociological introduction at the Open University*. London: Routledge

Partridge, E. (1950) *Here, There and Everywhere: essays on language*. London: Kegan Paul

Patel, N. (1990) *A Race Against Time*. London: Runnymede Trust

Payne, J. (1969) 'A Comparative Study of the Mental Ability of 7 and 8 year old British and West Indian Children in a West Midland Town'. *British Journal of Educational Psychology* 39

Pearson, M. (1990) *Millennial Dreams and Moral Dilemmas. Seventh Day Adventism and contemporary ethics.* Cambridge: Cambridge University Press

Phoenix, A. (1988) 'The Afro Caribbean Myth'. *New Society* 4th March p.10-13

Philips, T. C., (1980)'Black Backlash' *Times Educational Supplement*, 19th December

Pickering, W. (1970) Religion — a Leisure-time Pursuit? *A Sociological Year Book on Religion in Britain* pp.26-93 ed D Martin and M Hall. London: SCM Press

Pinkney, A. (1972) *Red, Black and Green. Black Nationalism in the United States.* Princeton: Princeton University Press

Plowden Report (1967) *Children and Their Primary Schools*. London: HMSO

Plummer, K. (1983) *Documents of Life*. London: Allen and Unwin

Price, K. (1979) *Endless Pressure*. Harmondsworth: Penguin

Poppleton and Pilkington (1963) The Measurement of Religious Attitudes in a University Population. *British Journal of Social Psychology* pp.20-36

Quirk, R. (1962) *The use of English.* London: Longman

Rampton (1981) *West Indians in our schools.* London: HMSO

Randall, F. (1986) *Sociology.* London: Pitman

Redbridge Community Relations Council and Black People's Progressive Association (1978) *Cause for concern: West Indian pupils in Redbridge*

Rex, J. and Moore, R. *et.al.* (1967) *Race, Community and Conflict: a study of Sparkbrook.* Oxfrd University Press.

Rex, J. and Tomlinson, S. (1979) *Colonial Immigrants in a British City — A Class Analysis*. London: Routledge and Kegan Paul

Robinson, C. J. (1983) *Black Marxism — the making of the black radical tradition*

Robinson, T. (1985) 'Some teachers are racist', *The Times Educational Supplement* 25 October

Rodney, (1972) *How Europe Underdeveloped Africa.* London: Bogle L'Overture

Rosenthal, R. and Jacobson, L. (1968) *Pygmalion in the Classroom.* New York: Holt, Rhinehart and Winston

Rowe, D. (1982) *The Construction of Life and Death.* London: Fontana Paperbacks

Rowe, D. (1987) *Beyond Fear.* London: Fontana Paperbacks

Rowe, D. (1989) *Death and Religion.* London: Fontana Paperbacks

Ryan, W. (1971) *Blaming the Victim.* London: Orbach and Chambers Ltd

Sacks, J. (1990) The Environment of Faith. Rieth Lectures 1. *The Listener*, 15 November 1990

Sargent, L. W. (1962) 'Occupational Status in a Religious Group' in *Review of Religious Research* Vol. 4 part 3 pp.149-153

Scarfe, A. and Sookhedeo, P. (1981) *Christianity and Marxism.* London: Paternoster Press

Schloredt, V. and Brown, P. (1988) *Martin Luther King.* Watford: Exley

Schulke, F. and McPhee, P. (1988) *King Remembered.* London: North and Co

Schwartz, G. (1972) *Sect Ideologies and Social Status*. Chicago: Chicago Press

Sertima, I. (ed) (1985) *Blacks in Science, Ancient and Modern*. London: Transaction Books

Sharpe, S. (1976) *Just Like a Girl: How Girls Learn to be Women*. Harmonds- worth: Penguin

Shuker, N. (1988) *Martin Luther King*. London: Burke

Sikes, P., Measor, L. and Woods, P. (1985) *Teachers' Crises: Courses and Continuities*. Lewis: Falmer Press

Slack, K. (1970) *Martin Luther King*. London: SCM Press Ltd

Smith, D. and Simpson, C. (1981) *Mugabe*. Glasgow: Sphere Books Ltd

Smith, D.J. (1977) Racial Disadvantage in Britain: the PEP Report. Harmondsworth: Penguin

Smith, D. J. and Tomlinson, S. (1989) *The school effect: A study of multiracial comprehensives*. London: Policy Studies Institute

St Clair Drake (1970) *The Redemption of African and Black Religion*. Chicago: Third World Press

Stenhouse, L. (1980) 'The study of samples and the study of cases'. *Bristol Educational Research Journal,* Vol. 6, No. 1, pp.106

Stokely, C. and Hamilton, C. V. (1967) *Black Power. The Politics of Liberation in America*. New York: Vintage Book

Stone, M. (1981) *The Education of the Black Child in Britain*. London: Fontana Paperbacks

Storey, M. (1970) '*Methods of Social Research*.' Oxford: Pergammon

Straughn, R. A. (1981) *Black Woman's Black Man's Guide to a Spiritual Union*. New York: Oracle of Thoth

Sutcliffe, D. (1982) *Black British English*. Oxford: Blackwell

Sutcliffe, D. and Wong, A. (1986) *The Language of Black Experience*. Oxford: Basil Blackwell Ltd

Swann, M. (1985) *Education for all*. Final Report of the Committee of Inquiry into the Education of Children from Ethnic Minority Groups, Cmnd 9453. London: HMSO

Taylor, M. J. (1981) *Caught Between — A Review of Research into the Education of Pupils of West Indian Origin*. Slough: NFER

Taylor, Y. (1992) 'Getting by without a Saviour', *Times Educational Supplement*. 24 April

Theobald, R. (1970) 'Seventh Day Adventists' *A Sociological Yearbook of Religion in Britain* pp.111-131

Thompson, D. C. (1963) *The Negro Leadership Class*. Prentice- Hall Inc

Tomlinson, S. (1981) *Educational subnormality: A study in decision making*. London: Routledge and Kegan Paul

Tomlinson, S. and Tomes, H. (1983) *Ethnic Minorities British Schools. A Review of the literature 1960-82*. London: Heinemann Educational Books

Trowler, P. (1986) *Topics in Sociology.* London: Bell and Hyman

Troyna, B. (1984) 'Fact or Artefact? The Educational Underachievement of Black Pupils', *British Journal of Sociology of Education* Vol. 5 No. 2, pp.153-66

Troyna, B. (1985) 'The great divide — policies and practices in multicultural education', *British Journal of Sociology of Education* Vol. 6 No. 2

Troyna, B. and Williams, J. (1986) *Racism, Education and the State.* London: Croom Helm

Venning, P. 'Menace Warning sent to Harringey heads over exam' *Times Education Supplement.* 11 Feb 1983

Verma, C. K. and Bagley, C. (1982) *Self concepts: Achievement Multicultural Education.* London: MacMillan

Wallis, R. (1984) *The Elementary forms of the new religious life.* London: Routledge and Kegan Paul

Walvin, J. (1973) *Black and White.* London: Heinemann

Ward, R. H. (1970) 'Some Aspects of Religious Life in an Immigrant Area of Manchester'. *Sociological Yearbook of Religion in Britain* pp.12-29

Webb, R. K. (1980) *Modern England from the 18th Century to the Present.* London: Allen and Unwin

Weber, M. (1971) 'The Protestant Ethic and the Spirit of Capitalism' in Thompson, and Tunstall, J. (eds) *Sociological perspectives, selected readings.* Harmondsworth Penguin in association with Open University Press, pp.408-13

Weber, M. (1965) *The Sociology of Religion.* London: Methuen

White, E. G. (1923) *Fundamentals of Christian Education.* Nashville: Southern Publishing Association

White E. G. (1952) *Education.* Nashville: Southern Publishing Association

White, E. G. (1971) *Mind Character and Personality* Vol 1 and 2. Nashville: Southern Publishing Association

Willems, E. C. (1969) 'Religious Pluralism and Class Structure', in Robertson and Roland (ed) *Sociology of Religion.* Brazil and Chile

Williams, C. (1988) *The Destruction of Black Civilization: Great issues of race from 4500 BC — 2000AD.* Chicago: Third World Press

Wilson, A. (1987) *Mixed Race Children: A Study of Identity.* London: Allen and Unwin

Wilson, B. R. (1959) 'An Analysis of Sect Development'. *American Sociological Review* Vol. 24 No. 1 pp.3-15

Wilson, B. R. (1961) *Sects and Society.* London: Heinemann

Wilson, B. R. (ed) (1967) *Patterns of Sectarianism. Organisation and ideologies, social and religious movements.* London: Heinemann

Wilson, B. R. (1969) 'A Typology of Sects' in Robertson, R. (eds) pp.361-83. *Sociology of Religion.* Harmondsworth: Penguin

Wilson, B. (1970) *Religious Sects.* London: Weidenfeld and Nicholson

Wilson, B. (1982) *Religion in Sociological Perspective.* Milton Keynes: Open University Press

Wolfson, N (1976) 'Speech events and natural speech: some implications for sociolinguistics methodology'. *Language in Society,* 5, pp. 189-209

Woods, P (1985) 'Conversation with teachers — some aspects of life history method'. *Education Research Journal,* Vol. 11, No. 1, pp.13-26

Woods, P. (1986) *Inside Schools, Ethnography in Educational Research.* London: Routledge and Kegan Paul

Wright, C. (1985b) 'Who succeeds at school and who decides?' *Multicultural Teaching*, Vol. 4, No. 1, autumn, pp.11-16

Wright, C. Y. (1988) The school experience of pupils of West Indian background. Unpublished PhD thesis, University of Keele

Yinger, J. Milton (1971) 'Types of Religious Organisations' in Thompson, and Tunstall, J. (eds) *Sociological perspectives, selected readings.* Harmondsworth Penguin in association with Open University Press, p.207

Zweig, F. (1948) *Labour, Life and Poverty.* London: Gollancz

Index